Salter Air Fryer Cookbook UK For Beginners

365 Crispy, Easy and Delicious Recipes for Beginners ans Advanced Users to Cook Your Favorite Food Easily

Ellie Gardner

All Rights Reserved.

The contents of this book may not be reproduced, copied or transmitted without the direct written permission of the author or publisher. Under no circumstances will the publisher or the author be held responsible or liable for any damage, compensation or pecuniary loss arising directly or indirectly from the information contained in this book.

Legal notice. This book is protected by copyright. It is intended for personal use only. You may not modify, distribute, sell, use, quote or paraphrase any part or content of this book without the consent of the author or publisher.

Notice Of Disclaimer.

Please note that the information in this document is intended for educational and entertainment purposes only. Every effort has been made to provide accurate, up-to-date, reliable and complete information. No warranty of any kind is declared or implied. The reader acknowledges that the author does not engage in the provision of legal, financial, medical or professional advice. The content in this book has been obtained from a variety of sources. Please consult a licensed professional before attempting any of the techniques described in this book. By reading this document, the reader agrees that in no event shall the author be liable for any direct or indirect damages, including but not limited to errors, omissions or inaccuracies, resulting from the use of the information in this document.

CONTENTS

TIPS FOR AIR FRYER SUCCESS

Know Your Appliance

First, and most important, read your appliance manual. All air fryers are not created equal. Features differ among models. Even timers work differently. Parts of some air fryers may be dishwasher safe, but you may have to hand-wash others. Any misuse of your air fryer or its parts could void the warranty. Read all safety information, and never use the machine in any way that violates the manufacturer's instructions for safe use. In addition to keeping you safe, your manual should provide details about your model's features and functions. Most of us hate reading instructions or manuals, but it's worth taking the time to understand how to use it. Sometimes that can make all the difference between frustration and success.

Cooking Time

Many factors can affect cooking times, including size, volume, and temperature of food, thickness of breading, and so on. Even your local humidity levels can affect required cooking times. Wattage is another factor. All recipes in this cookbook were tested in 1,425-watt air fryers. A unit with a higher or lower wattage may cook somewhat faster or slower. For most recipes, total cooking time shouldn't vary by more than a minute or two, but to avoid overcooking, check food early and often. Always start with the shortest cooking time listed in a recipe. Check for doneness at that point and continue cooking if necessary. When you try a recipe for the first time and the minimum cooking time is, say, 20 minutes or longer, check the dish at about 15 minutes just to be safe. If you're new to air frying, don't be afraid to pause your air fryer often to open the drawer and check foods. That's the best way to save dinner before it overcooks or burns.

Minimum Temperatures for Food Safety

Consuming raw or undercooked eggs, fish, game, meats, poultry, seafood, or shellfish may increase your risk of foodborne illness. To ensure that foods are safe to eat, ground beef, lamb, pork, and veal should be cooked to a minimum of 75°C/160°F. Other cuts of these meats such as beef steaks should be cooked to at least 65°C/145°F. All turkey and chicken should be cooked to a minimum of 75°C/165°F.

Cooking in Batches

For best results, always cut foods into uniform pieces so they cook more evenly. Follow recipes to know whether foods can be stacked or must cook in a single layer. Directions will indicate whether you need to turn or shake the basket to redistribute foods during cooking. All recipes developed for this cookbook were tested in air fryers with an interior capacity of approximately 3 quarts. Using these "standard"-size air fryers often requires cooking in two batches, but many foods cook so quickly that this additional cooking time doesn't matter.

For foods that require lengthy cooking time, the first batch may cool too much while the second batch is cooking, but the solution is simple. Air fryers do an excellent job of reheating foods. Right before your second batch finishes cooking, place your first batch on top so it reheats for serving. If there's not enough room in your air fryer basket, wait until the second batch is done, remove it, and reheat the first batch for a minute or two. Keep this strategy in mind any time you need to heat up leftovers. They come out hot and crispy—unlike microwave-reheated foods, which can feel soggy, rubbery, or tough.

You can also buy a larger air fryer. Some models have a capacity of approximately 5 quarts. If you have an air fryer of this size, you may be able to cook many of our recipes in a single batch. Follow recipe instructions as to whether a particular food can be crowded or stacked, and fill the basket accordingly. You may need to adjust recipe times slightly, but after cooking a few recipes, you'll know how to judge that.

Smoking

Select a suitable location for your unit. If possible, place it near your range so you can use the vent hood if needed. Follow the manufacturer's instructions to protect your countertop and to allow the required amount of open space around the back, sides, and top of your air fryer. Smoking isn't a frequent problem but does occur when cooking meats or other foods with a high fat content. Adding water to the air fryer drawer can help sometimes but not always. Coconut, for example, tends to smoke no matter what. An accumulation of grease in the bottom of your air fryer can also cause smoking. Prevent this problem by keeping the drawer clean and free of food or fat buildup.

Excessive smoking, especially black smoke, is not normal. This could result from an electrical malfunction, in which case unplug your appliance immediately and contact the manufacturer.

Bread And Breakfast

Pumpkin Loaf

Servings: 6
Cooking Time: 22 Minutes
Ingredients:

- cooking spray
- 1 large egg
- ½ cup granulated sugar
- ⅓ cup oil
- ½ cup canned pumpkin (not pie filling)
- ½ teaspoon vanilla
- ⅔ cup flour plus 1 tablespoon
- ½ teaspoon baking powder
- ½ teaspoon baking soda
- ½ teaspoon salt
- 1 teaspoon pumpkin pie spice
- ¼ teaspoon cinnamon

Directions:

1. Spray 6 x 6-inch baking dish lightly with cooking spray.
2. Place baking dish in air fryer basket and preheat air fryer to 330°F.
3. In a large bowl, beat eggs and sugar together with a hand mixer.
4. Add oil, pumpkin, and vanilla and mix well.
5. Sift together all dry ingredients. Add to pumpkin mixture and beat well, about 1 minute.
6. Pour batter in baking dish and cook at 330°F for 22 minutes or until toothpick inserted in center of loaf comes out clean.

Bacon, Broccoli And Swiss Cheese Bread Pudding

Servings: 2
Cooking Time: 48 Minutes
Ingredients:

- ½ pound thick cut bacon, cut into ¼-inch pieces
- 3 cups brioche bread or rolls, cut into ½-inch cubes
- 3 eggs
- 1 cup milk
- ½ teaspoon salt
- freshly ground black pepper
- 1 cup frozen broccoli florets, thawed and chopped
- 1½ cups grated Swiss cheese

Directions:

1. Preheat the air fryer to 400°F.
2. Air-fry the bacon for 6 minutes until crispy, shaking the basket a few times while it cooks to help it cook evenly. Remove the bacon and set it aside on a paper towel.
3. Air-fry the brioche bread cubes for 2 minutes to dry and toast lightly. (If your brioche is a few days old and slightly stale, you can omit this step.)
4. Butter a 6- or 7-inch cake pan. Combine all the ingredients in a large bowl and toss well. Transfer the mixture to the buttered cake pan, cover with aluminum foil and refrigerate the bread pudding overnight, or for at least 8 hours.
5. Remove the casserole from the refrigerator an hour before you plan to cook, and let it sit on the countertop to come to room temperature.
6. Preheat the air fryer to 330°F. Transfer the covered cake pan, to the basket of the air fryer, lowering the dish into the basket using a sling made of aluminum foil (fold a piece of aluminum foil into a strip about 2-inches wide by 24-inches long). Fold the ends of the aluminum foil over the top of the dish before returning the basket to the air fryer. Air-fry for 20 minutes. Remove the foil and air-fry for an additional 20 minutes. If the top starts to brown a little too much before the custard has set, simply return the foil to the pan. The bread pudding has cooked through when a skewer inserted into the center comes out clean.

Viking Toast

Servings: 2
Cooking Time: 20 Minutes
Ingredients:

- 2 tbsp minced green chili pepper
- 1 avocado, pressed
- 1 clove garlic, minced
- ¼ tsp lemon juice
- Salt and pepper to taste
- 2 bread slices
- 2 plum tomatoes, sliced
- 4 oz smoked salmon
- ¼ diced peeled red onion

Directions:

1. Preheat air fryer at 350ºF. Combine the avocado, garlic, lemon juice, and salt in a bowl until you reach your desired consistency. Spread avocado mixture on the bread slices.
2. Top with tomato slices and sprinkle with black pepper. Place bread slices in the frying basket and Bake for 5 minutes. Transfer to a plate. Top each bread slice with salmon, green chili pepper, and red onion. Serve.

Breakfast Chimichangas

Servings: 4
Cooking Time: 8 Minutes
Ingredients:

- Four 8-inch flour tortillas
- ½ cup canned refried beans
- 1 cup scrambled eggs
- ½ cup grated cheddar or Monterey jack cheese
- 1 tablespoon vegetable oil
- 1 cup salsa

Directions:

1. Lay the flour tortillas out flat on a cutting board. In the center of each tortilla, spread 2 tablespoons refried beans. Next, add ¼ cup eggs and 2 tablespoons cheese to each tortilla.
2. To fold the tortillas, begin on the left side and fold to the center. Then fold the right side into the center. Next fold the bottom and top down and roll over to completely seal the chimichanga. Using a pastry brush or oil mister, brush the tops of the tortilla packages with oil.
3. Preheat the air fryer to 400°F for 4 minutes. Place the chimichangas into the air fryer basket, seam side down, and air fry for 4 minutes. Using tongs, turn over the chimichangas and cook for an additional 2 to 3 minutes or until light golden brown.

Sugar-dusted Beignets

Servings: 4
Cooking Time: 30 Minutes
Ingredients:

- 1 tsp fast active dry yeast
- 1/3 cup buttermilk
- 3 tbsp brown sugar
- 1 egg
- ½ tsp brandy
- 1 ½ cups flour
- 3 tbsp chopped dried plums
- 3 tbsp golden raisins
- 2 tbsp butter, melted
- 2 tbsp powdered sugar

Directions:

1. Combine the yeast with 3 tbsp of water and leave it until frothy, about 5 minutes. Add the buttermilk, brown sugar, brandy, and egg and stir. Add the flour and stir again. Use your hands to mix the plums and raisins into the dough. Leave the mix in the bowl for 15 minutes.
2. Preheat air fryer to 330°F. Shape the dough in a square, then slice it into 16 pieces. Make 16 balls, then drizzle butter over the balls. Put the balls in the air fryer in a single layer, making sure they don't touch. Air Fry for 5-8 minutes until they puff up and are golden. Repeat until all balls are cooked. Toss in powdered sugar and serve.

Mini Everything Bagels

Servings: 4
Cooking Time: 6 Minutes
Ingredients:

- 1 cup all-purpose flour
- 2 teaspoons baking powder
- ½ teaspoon salt
- 1 cup plain Greek yogurt
- 1 egg, whisked
- 1 teaspoon sesame seeds
- 1 teaspoon dehydrated onions
- ½ teaspoon poppy seeds
- ½ teaspoon garlic powder
- ½ teaspoon sea salt flakes

Directions:

1. In a large bowl, mix together the flour, baking powder, and salt. Make a well in the dough and add in the Greek yogurt. Mix with a spoon until a dough forms.
2. Place the dough onto a heavily floured surface and knead for 3 minutes. You may use up to 1 cup of additional flour as you knead the dough, if necessary.
3. Cut the dough into 8 pieces and roll each piece into a 6-inch, snakelike piece. Touch the ends of each piece together

so it closes the circle and forms a bagel shape. Brush the tops of the bagels with the whisked egg.

4. In a small bowl, combine the sesame seeds, dehydrated onions, poppy seeds, garlic powder, and sea salt flakes. Sprinkle the seasoning on top of the bagels.

5. Preheat the air fryer to 360°F. Using a bench scraper or flat-edged spatula, carefully place the bagels into the air fryer basket. Spray the bagel tops with cooking spray. Air-fry the bagels for 6 minutes or until golden brown. Allow the bread to cool at least 10 minutes before slicing for serving.

Shakshuka Cups

Servings: 4

Cooking Time: 25 Minutes

Ingredients:

- 2 tbsp tomato paste
- ½ cup chicken broth
- 4 tomatoes, diced
- 2 garlic cloves, minced
- ½ tsp dried oregano
- ½ tsp dried coriander
- ½ tsp dried basil
- ¼ tsp red pepper flakes
- ¼ tsp paprika
- 4 eggs
- Salt and pepper to taste
- 2 scallions, diced
- ½ cup grated cheddar cheese
- ½ cup Parmesan cheese
- 4 bread slices, toasted

Directions:

1. Preheat air fryer to 350°F. Combine the tomato paste, chicken broth, tomatoes, garlic, oregano, coriander, basil, red pepper flakes, and paprika. Pour the mixture evenly into greased ramekins. Bake in the air fryer for 5 minutes. Carefully remove the ramekins and crack one egg in each ramekin, then season with salt and pepper. Top with scallions, grated cheese, and Parmesan cheese. Return the ramekins to the frying basket and bake for 3-5 minutes until the eggs are set, and the cheese is melted. Serve with toasted bread immediately.

Classic Cinnamon Rolls

Servings: 4

Cooking Time: 6 Minutes

Ingredients:

- 1½ cups all-purpose flour
- 1 tablespoon granulated sugar
- 2 teaspoons baking powder
- ½ teaspoon salt
- 4 tablespoons butter, divided
- ½ cup buttermilk
- 2 tablespoons brown sugar
- 1 teaspoon cinnamon
- 1 cup powdered sugar
- 2 tablespoons milk

Directions:

1. Preheat the air fryer to 360°F.
2. In a large bowl, stir together the flour, sugar, baking powder, and salt. Cut in 3 tablespoons of the butter with a pastry blender or two knives until coarse crumbs remain. Stir in the buttermilk until a dough forms.
3. Place the dough onto a floured surface and roll out into a square shape about ½ inch thick.
4. Melt the remaining 1 tablespoon of butter in the microwave for 20 seconds. Using a pastry brush or your fingers, spread the melted butter onto the dough.
5. In a small bowl, mix together the brown sugar and cinnamon. Sprinkle the mixture across the surface of the dough. Roll the dough up, forming a long log. Using a pastry cutter or sharp knife, cut 10 cinnamon rolls.
6. Carefully place the cinnamon rolls into the air fryer basket. Then bake at 360°F for 6 minutes or until golden brown.
7. Meanwhile, in a small bowl, whisk together the powdered sugar and milk.
8. Plate the cinnamon rolls and drizzle the glaze over the surface before serving.

Cinnamon-coconut Doughnuts

Servings: 6

Cooking Time: 35 Minutes

Ingredients:

- 1 egg, beaten
- ¼ cup milk
- 2 tbsp safflower oil
- 1 ½ tsp vanilla
- ½ tsp lemon zest
- 1 ½ cups all-purpose flour
- ¾ cup coconut sugar
- 2 ½ tsp cinnamon
- ½ tsp ground nutmeg
- ¼ tsp salt
- ¾ tsp baking powder

Directions:

1. Preheat air fryer to 350°F. Add the egg, milk, oil, vanilla, and lemon zest. Stir well and set this wet mixture aside.In a different bowl, combine the flour, ½ cup coconut sugar, ½ teaspoon cinnamon, nutmeg, salt, and baking powder. Stir well. Add this mixture to the wet mix and blend. Pull off bits of the dough and roll into balls.
2. Place in the greased frying basket, leaving room between as they get bigger. Spray the tops with oil and Air Fry for 8-10 minutes, flipping once. During the last 2 minutes of frying, place 4 tbsp of coconut sugar and 2 tsp of cinnamon in a bowl and stir to combine. After frying, coat each donut by spraying with oil and toss in the cinnamon-sugar mix. Serve and enjoy!

Pancake Muffins

Servings: 4

Cooking Time: 8 Minutes

Ingredients:

- 1 cup flour
- 2 tablespoons sugar (optional)
- ½ teaspoon baking soda
- 1 teaspoon baking powder
- ¼ teaspoon salt
- 1 egg, beaten
- 1 cup buttermilk
- 2 tablespoons melted butter
- 1 teaspoon pure vanilla extract
- 24 foil muffin cups
- cooking spray
- Suggested Fillings
- 1 teaspoon of jelly or fruit preserves
- 1 tablespoon or less fresh blueberries; chopped fresh strawberries; chopped frozen cherries; dark chocolate chips; chopped walnuts, pecans, or other nuts; cooked, crumbled bacon or sausage

Directions:

1. In a large bowl, stir together flour, optional sugar, baking soda, baking powder, and salt.
2. In a small bowl, combine egg, buttermilk, butter, and vanilla. Mix well.
3. Pour egg mixture into dry ingredients and stir to mix well but don't overbeat.
4. Double up the muffin cups and remove the paper liners from the top cups. Spray the foil cups lightly with cooking spray.
5. Place 6 sets of muffin cups in air fryer basket. Pour just enough batter into each cup to cover the bottom. Sprinkle with desired filling. Pour in more batter to cover the filling and fill the cups about ¾ full.
6. Cook at 330°F for 8minutes.
7. Repeat steps 5 and 6 for the remaining 6 pancake muffins.

Breakfast Pot Pies

Servings: 4

Cooking Time: 20 Minutes

Ingredients:

- 1 refrigerated pie crust
- ½ pound pork breakfast sausage
- ¼ cup diced onion
- 1 garlic clove, minced
- ½ teaspoon ground black pepper
- ¼ teaspoon salt
- 1 cup chopped bell peppers
- 1 cup roasted potatoes
- 2 cups milk
- 2 to 3 tablespoons all-purpose flour

Directions:

1. Flatten the store-bought pie crust out on an even surface. Cut 4 equal circles that are slightly larger than the circumference of ramekins (by about ¼ inch). Set aside.
2. In a medium pot, sauté the breakfast sausage with the onion, garlic, black pepper, and salt. When browned, add in the bell peppers and potatoes and cook an additional 3 to 4 minutes to soften the bell peppers. Remove from the heat and portion equally into the ramekins.
3. To the same pot (without washing it), add the milk. Heat over medium-high heat until boiling. Slowly reduce to a simmer and stir in the flour, 1 tablespoon at a time, until the gravy thickens and coats the back of a wooden spoon (about 5 minutes).
4. Remove from the heat and equally portion ½ cup of gravy into each ramekin on top of the sausage and potato mixture.
5. Place the circle pie crusts on top of the ramekins, lightly pressing them down on the perimeter of each ramekin with the prongs of a fork. Gently poke the prongs into the center top of the pie crust a few times to create holes for the steam to escape as the pie cooks.
6. Bake in the air fryer for 6 minutes (or until the tops are golden brown).
7. Remove and let cool 5 minutes before serving.

Carrot Muffins

Servings: 4
Cooking Time: 35 Minutes + Cooling Time
Ingredients:

- 1 ½ cups flour
- ½ tsp baking soda
- ½ tsp baking powder
- 1/3 cup brown sugar
- ½ tsp ground cinnamon
- 2 eggs
- 2/3 cup almond milk
- 3 tbsp sunflower oil
- ½ cup shredded carrots
- 1/3 cup golden raisins

Directions:

1. Preheat air fryer to 320°F. Mix the flour, baking powder, baking soda, brown sugar, and cinnamon in a bowl. In a smaller bowl, whisk the eggs, almond milk, and oil. Combine the mixtures, stir, but leave some lumps in the batter. Add the carrots and raisins and stir. Make 8 foil muffin cups by doubling 16 cups. Set 4 cups in the air fryer and put the batter in the cups until they're ¾ full. Bake in the fryer for 13-17 minutes; the muffin tops should bounce when touched. Repeat until all muffins are done. Let the muffins cool on a rack, then serve.

Oat Muffins With Blueberries

Servings: 6
Cooking Time: 25 Minutes
Ingredients:

- ¾ cup old-fashioned rolled oats
- 1 ½ cups flour
- ½ cup evaporated cane sugar
- 1 tbsp baking powder
- 1 tsp ground cinnamon
- ¼ tsp ground chia seeds
- ¼ tsp ground sesame seeds
- ½ tsp salt
- 1 cup vanilla almond milk
- 4 tbsp butter, softened
- 2 eggs
- 1 tsp vanilla extract
- 1 cup blueberries
- 2 tbsp powdered sugar

Directions:

1. Preheat air fryer to 350°F. Combine flour oats, sugar, baking powder, chia seeds, sesame seeds, cinnamon, and salt in a bowl. Mix the almond milk, butter, eggs, and vanilla in another bowl until smooth. Pour in dry ingredients and stir to combine. Fold in blueberries.Fill 12 silicone muffin cups about halfway and place them in the frying basket. Bake for 12-15 minutes until just browned, and a toothpick in the center comes out clean. Cool for 5 minutes. Serve topped with powdered sugar.

Seasoned Herbed Sourdough Croutons

Servings: 4
Cooking Time: 7 Minutes
Ingredients:

- 4 cups cubed sourdough bread, 1-inch cubes (about 8 ounces)
- 1 tablespoon olive oil
- 1 teaspoon fresh thyme leaves
- ¼ – ½ teaspoon salt
- freshly ground black pepper

Directions:

1. Combine all ingredients in a bowl and taste to make sure it is seasoned to your liking.
2. Preheat the air fryer to 400°F.
3. Toss the bread cubes into the air fryer and air-fry for 7 minutes, shaking the basket once or twice while they cook.
4. Serve warm or store in an airtight container.

White Wheat Walnut Bread

Servings: 8
Cooking Time: 25 Minutes
Ingredients:

- 1 cup lukewarm water (105–115°F)
- 1 packet RapidRise yeast
- 1 tablespoon light brown sugar
- 2 cups whole-grain white wheat flour
- 1 egg, room temperature, beaten with a fork
- 2 teaspoons olive oil
- ½ teaspoon salt
- ½ cup chopped walnuts
- cooking spray

Directions:

1. In a small bowl, mix the water, yeast, and brown sugar.
2. Pour yeast mixture over flour and mix until smooth.
3. Add the egg, olive oil, and salt and beat with a wooden spoon for 2minutes.
4. Stir in chopped walnuts. You will have very thick batter rather than stiff bread dough.
5. Spray air fryer baking pan with cooking spray and pour in batter, smoothing the top.
6. Let batter rise for 15minutes.
7. Preheat air fryer to 360°F.
8. Cook bread for 25 minutes, until toothpick pushed into center comes out with crumbs clinging. Let bread rest for 10minutes before removing from pan.

Bread Boat Eggs

Servings: 4
Cooking Time: 10 Minutes
Ingredients:

- 4 pistolette rolls
- 1 teaspoon butter
- ¼ cup diced fresh mushrooms
- ½ teaspoon dried onion flakes
- 4 eggs
- ½ teaspoon salt
- ¼ teaspoon dried dill weed
- ¼ teaspoon dried parsley
- 1 tablespoon milk

Directions:

1. Cut a rectangle in the top of each roll and scoop out center, leaving ½-inch shell on the sides and bottom.
2. Place butter, mushrooms, and dried onion in air fryer baking pan and cook for 1 minute. Stir and cook 3 moreminutes.
3. In a medium bowl, beat together the eggs, salt, dill, parsley, and milk. Pour mixture into pan with mushrooms.
4. Cook at 390°F for 2minutes. Stir. Continue cooking for 3 or 4minutes, stirring every minute, until eggs are scrambled to your liking.
5. Remove baking pan from air fryer and fill rolls with scrambled egg mixture.
6. Place filled rolls in air fryer basket and cook at 390°F for 2 to 3minutes or until rolls are lightly browned.

Cheddar-ham-corn Muffins

Servings: 8

Cooking Time: 8 Minutes

Ingredients:

- ¾ cup yellow cornmeal
- ¼ cup flour
- 1½ teaspoons baking powder
- ¼ teaspoon salt
- 1 egg, beaten
- 2 tablespoons canola oil
- ½ cup milk
- ½ cup shredded sharp Cheddar cheese
- ½ cup diced ham
- 8 foil muffin cups, liners removed and sprayed with cooking spray

Directions:

1. Preheat air fryer to 390°F.
2. In a medium bowl, stir together the cornmeal, flour, baking powder, and salt.
3. Add egg, oil, and milk to dry ingredients and mix well.
4. Stir in shredded cheese and diced ham.
5. Divide batter among the muffin cups.
6. Place 4 filled muffin cups in air fryer basket and bake for 5minutes.
7. Reduce temperature to 330°F and bake for 1 to 2minutes or until toothpick inserted in center of muffin comes out clean.
8. Repeat steps 6 and 7 to cook remaining muffins.

Fried Pb&j

Servings: 4

Cooking Time: 8 Minutes

Ingredients:

- ½ cup cornflakes, crushed
- ¼ cup shredded coconut
- 8 slices oat nut bread or any whole-grain, oversize bread
- 6 tablespoons peanut butter
- 2 medium bananas, cut into ½-inch-thick slices
- 6 tablespoons pineapple preserves
- 1 egg, beaten
- oil for misting or cooking spray

Directions:

1. Preheat air fryer to 360°F.
2. In a shallow dish, mix together the cornflake crumbs and coconut.
3. For each sandwich, spread one bread slice with 1½ tablespoons of peanut butter. Top with banana slices. Spread another bread slice with 1½ tablespoons of preserves. Combine to make a sandwich.
4. Using a pastry brush, brush top of sandwich lightly with beaten egg. Sprinkle with about 1½ tablespoons of crumb coating, pressing it in to make it stick. Spray with oil.
5. Turn sandwich over and repeat to coat and spray the other side.
6. Cooking 2 at a time, place sandwiches in air fryer basket and cook for 6 to 7minutes or until coating is golden brown and crispy. If sandwich doesn't brown enough, spray with a little more oil and cook at 390°F for another minute.
7. Cut cooked sandwiches in half and serve warm.

Egg & Bacon Toasts

Servings: 4

Cooking Time: 25 Minutes

Ingredients:

- 4 French bread slices, cut diagonally
- 1 + tsp butter
- 4 eggs
- 2 tbsp milk
- ½ tsp dried thyme
- Salt and pepper to taste
- 4 oz cooked bacon, crumbled
- 2/3 cup grated Colby cheese

Directions:

1. Preheat the air fryer to 350°F. Spray each slice of bread with oil and Bake in the frying basket for 2-3 minutes until light brown; set aside. Beat together the eggs, milk, thyme, salt, and pepper in a bowl and add the melted butter. Transfer to a 6-inch cake pan and place the pan into the fryer. Bake for 7-8 minutes, stirring once or until the eggs are set. Transfer the egg mixture into a bowl.
2. Top the bread slices with egg mixture, bacon, and cheese. Return to the fryer and Bake for 4-8 minutes or until the cheese melts and browns in spots. Serve.

Morning Chicken Frittata Cups

Servings:6

Cooking Time: 30 Minutes

Ingredients:

- ¼ cup shredded cooked chicken breasts
- 3 eggs
- 2 tbsp heavy cream
- 4 tsp Tabasco sauce
- ¼ cup grated Asiago cheese
- 2 tbsp chives, chopped

Directions:

1. Preheat air fryer to 350ºF. Beat all ingredients in a bowl. Divide the egg mixture between greased 6 muffin cups and place them in the frying basket. Bake for 8-10 minutes until set. Let cool slightly before serving. Enjoy!

Egg & Bacon Pockets

Servings: 4

Cooking Time: 50 Minutes

Ingredients:

- 2 tbsp olive oil
- 4 bacon slices, chopped
- ¼ red bell pepper, diced
- 1/3 cup scallions, chopped
- 4 eggs, beaten
- 1/3 cup grated Swiss cheese
- 1 cup flour
- 1 ½ tsp baking powder
- ½ tsp salt
- 1 cup Greek yogurt
- 1 egg white, beaten
- 2 tsp Italian seasoning
- 1 tbsp Tabasco sauce

Directions:

1. Warm the olive oil in a skillet over medium heat and add the bacon. Stir-fry for 3-4 minutes or until crispy. Add the bell pepper and scallions and sauté for 3-4 minutes. Pour in the beaten eggs and stir-fry to scramble them, 3 minutes. Stir in the Swiss cheese and set aside to cool.
2. Sift the flour, baking powder, and salt in a bowl. Add yogurt and mix together until combined. Transfer the dough to a floured workspace. Knead it for 3 minutes or until smooth. Form the dough into 4 equal balls. Roll out the balls into round discs. Divide the bacon-egg mixture between the rounds. Fold the dough over the filling and seal the edges with a fork. Brush the pockets with egg white and sprinkle with Italian seasoning.
3. Preheat air fryer to 350°F. Arrange the pockets on the greased frying basket and Bake for 9-11 minutes, flipping once until golden. Serve with Tabasco sauce.

Brown Sugar Grapefruit

Servings: 2

Cooking Time: 4 Minutes

Ingredients:

- 1 grapefruit
- 2 to 4 teaspoons brown sugar

Directions:

1. Preheat the air fryer to 400°F.
2. While the air fryer is Preheating, cut the grapefruit in half horizontally (in other words not through the stem or blossom end of the grapefruit). Slice the bottom of the grapefruit to help it sit flat on the counter if necessary. Using a sharp paring knife (serrated is great), cut around the grapefruit between the flesh of the fruit and the peel. Then, cut each segment away from the membrane so that it is sitting freely in the fruit.
3. Sprinkle 1 to 2 teaspoons of brown sugar on each half of the prepared grapefruit. Set up a rack in the air fryer basket (use an air fryer rack or make your own rack with some crumpled up aluminum foil). You don't have to use a rack, but doing so will get the grapefruit closer to the element so that the brown sugar can caramelize a little better. Transfer the grapefruit half to the rack in the air fryer basket. Depending on how big your grapefruit are and what size air fryer you have, you may need to do each half separately to make sure they sit flat.
4. Air-fry at 400°F for 4 minutes.
5. Remove and let it cool for just a minute before enjoying.

Egg And Sausage Crescent Rolls

Servings: 8
Cooking Time: 11 Minutes
Ingredients:

- 5 large eggs
- ¼ teaspoon black pepper
- ¼ teaspoon salt
- 1 tablespoon milk
- ¼ cup shredded cheddar cheese
- One 8-ounce package refrigerated crescent rolls
- 4 tablespoon pesto sauce
- 8 fully cooked breakfast sausage links, defrosted

Directions:

1. Preheat the air fryer to 320°F.
2. In a medium bowl, crack the eggs and whisk with the pepper, salt, and milk. Pour into a frying pan over medium heat and scramble. Just before the eggs are done, turn off the heat and add in the cheese. Continue to cook until the cheese has melted and the eggs are finished (about 5 minutes total). Remove from the heat.
3. Remove the crescent rolls from the package and press them flat onto a clean surface lightly dusted with flour. Add 1½ teaspoons of pesto sauce across the center of each roll. Place equal portions of eggs across all 8 rolls. Then top each roll with a sausage link and roll the dough up tight so it resembles the crescent-roll shape.
4. Lightly spray your air fryer basket with olive oil mist and place the rolls on top. Bake for 6 minutes or until the tops of the rolls are lightly browned.
5. Remove and let cool 3 to 5 minutes before serving.

Effortless Toffee Zucchini Bread

Servings: 6
Cooking Time: 30 Minutes
Ingredients:

- 1 cup flour
- ½ tsp baking soda
- ½ cup granulated sugar
- ¼ tsp ground cinnamon
- ¼ tsp nutmeg
- ¼ tsp salt
- 1/3 cup grated zucchini
- 1 egg
- 1 tbsp olive oil
- 1 tsp vanilla extract
- 2 tbsp English toffee bits
- 2 tbsp mini chocolate chips
- 1/2 cup chopped walnuts

Directions:

1. Preheat air fryer at 375°F. Combine the flour, baking soda, toffee bits, sugar, cinnamon, nutmeg, salt, zucchini, egg, olive oil, vanilla and chocolate chips in a bowl. Add the walnuts to the batter and mix until evenly distributed.
2. Pour the mixture into a greased cake pan. Place the pan in the fryer and Bake for 20 minutes. Let sit for 10 minutes until slightly cooled before slicing. Serve immediately.

Cinnamon Banana Bread With Pecans

Servings: 6
Cooking Time: 35 Minutes
Ingredients:

- 2 ripe bananas, mashed
- 1 egg
- ¼ cup Greek yogurt
- ¼ cup olive oil
- ½ tsp peppermint extract
- 2 tbsp honey
- 1 cup flour
- ¼ tsp salt
- ¼ tsp baking soda
- ½ tsp ground cinnamon
- ¼ cup chopped pecans

Directions:

1. Preheat air fryer to 360°F. Add the bananas, egg, yogurt, olive oil, peppermint, and honey in a large bowl and mix until combined and mostly smooth.
2. Sift the flour, salt, baking soda, and cinnamon into the wet mixture, then stir until just combined. Gently fold in the pecans. Spread to distribute evenly into a greased loaf pan. Place the loaf pan in the frying basket and Bake for 23 minutes or until golden brown on top and a toothpick inserted into the center comes out clean. Allow to cool for 5 minutes. Serve.

Egg Muffins

Servings: 4

Cooking Time: 11 Minutes

Ingredients:

- 4 eggs
- salt and pepper
- olive oil
- 4 English muffins, split
- 1 cup shredded Colby Jack cheese
- 4 slices ham or Canadian bacon

Directions:

1. Preheat air fryer to 390°F.
2. Beat together eggs and add salt and pepper to taste. Spray air fryer baking pan lightly with oil and add eggs. Cook for 2minutes, stir, and continue cooking for 4minutes, stirring every minute, until eggs are scrambled to your preference. Remove pan from air fryer.
3. Place bottom halves of English muffins in air fryer basket. Take half of the shredded cheese and divide it among the muffins. Top each with a slice of ham and one-quarter of the eggs. Sprinkle remaining cheese on top of the eggs. Use a fork to press the cheese into the egg a little so it doesn't slip off before it melts.
4. Cook at 360°F for 1 minute. Add English muffin tops and cook for 4minutes to heat through and toast the muffins.

Parsley Egg Scramble With Cottage Cheese

Servings:2

Cooking Time: 15 Minutes

Ingredients:

- 1 tbsp cottage cheese, crumbled
- 4 eggs
- Salt and pepper to taste
- 2 tsp heavy cream
- 1 tbsp chopped parsley

Directions:

1. Preheat air fryer to 400ºF. Grease a baking pan with olive oil. Beat the eggs, salt, and pepper in a bowl. Pour it into the pan, place the pan in the frying basket, and Air Fry for 5 minutes. Using a silicone spatula, stir in heavy cream, cottage cheese, and half of parsley and Air Fry for another 2 minutes. Scatter with parsley to serve.

Cream Cheese Deviled Eggs

Servings: 4

Cooking Time: 20 Minutes

Ingredients:

- 2 cooked bacon slices, crumbled
- 4 whole eggs
- 2 tbsp mayonnaise
- 1 tsp yellow mustard
- ½ tsp dill pickle juice
- 1 tsp diced sweet pickles
- Salt and pepper to taste
- 2 tbsp cream cheese
- Parsley for sprinkling

Directions:

1. Preheat air fryer at 250ºF. Place egg in the frying basket and Air Fry for 15 minutes. Then place them immediately into a bowl with ice and 1 cup of water to stop the cooking process. Let chill for 5 minutes, then carefully peel them. Cut egg in half lengthwise and spoon yolks into a bowl. Arrange the egg white halves on a plate.
2. Mash egg yolks with a fork. Stir in mayonnaise, mustard, pickle juice, diced pickles, salt, pepper and cream cheese. Pour 1 tbsp of the mixture into egg white halves, scatter with crumbled bacon and parsley and serve.

Crunchy Granola Muffins

Servings:4
Cooking Time: 15 Minutes

Ingredients:

- 1 cup walnut pieces
- 1 cup sunflower seeds
- 1 cup coconut flakes
- ¼ cup granulated sugar
- ⅛ cup coconut flour
- ⅛ cup pecan flour
- 2 tsp ground cinnamon
- 2 tbsp melted butter
- 2 tbsp almond butter
- ⅛ tsp salt

Directions:

1. Preheat air fryer to 300ºF. In a bowl, mix the walnuts, sunflower seeds, coconut flakes, sugar, coconut flour, pecan flour, cinnamon, butter, almond butter, and salt.
2. Spoon the mixture into an ungreased round 4-cup baking dish. Place it in the frying basket and Bake for 6 minutes, stirring once. Transfer to an airtight container, let cool for 10 minutes, then cover and store at room temperature until ready to serve.

Appetizers And Snacks

Panko-breaded Onion Rings

Servings: 4
Cooking Time: 12 Minutes

Ingredients:

- 1 large sweet onion, cut into ½-inch slices and rings separated
- 2 cups ice water
- ½ cup all-purpose flour
- 1 teaspoon paprika
- 1 teaspoon salt
- ½ teaspoon black pepper
- ½ teaspoon garlic powder
- ¼ teaspoon onion powder
- 1 egg, whisked
- 2 tablespoons milk
- 1 cup breadcrumbs

Directions:

1. Preheat the air fryer to 400°F.
2. In a large bowl, soak the onion rings in the water for 5 minutes. Drain and pat dry with a towel.
3. In a medium bowl, place the flour, paprika, salt, pepper, garlic powder, and onion powder.
4. In a second bowl, whisk together the egg and milk.
5. In a third bowl, place the breadcrumbs.
6. To bread the onion rings, dip them first into the flour mixture, then into the egg mixture (shaking off the excess), and then into the breadcrumbs. Place the coated onion rings onto a plate while you bread all the rings.
7. Place the onion rings into the air fryer basket in a single layer, sometimes nesting smaller rings into larger rings. Spray with cooking spray. Cook for 3 minutes, turn the rings over, and spray with more cooking spray. Cook for another 3 to 5 minutes. Cook the rings in batches; you may need to do 2 or 3 batches, depending on the size of your air fryer.

Sausage And Cheese Rolls

Servings: 3
Cooking Time: 18 Minutes

Ingredients:

- 3 3- to 3½-ounce sweet or hot Italian sausage links
- 2 1-ounce string cheese stick(s), unwrapped and cut in half lengthwise
- Three quarters from one thawed sheet (cut the sheet into four quarters; wrap and refreeze one of them) A 17.25-ounce box frozen puff pastry

Directions:

1. Preheat the air fryer to 400°F.
2. When the machine is at temperature, set the sausage links in the basket and air-fry undisturbed for 12 minutes, or until cooked through.
3. Use kitchen tongs to transfer the links to a wire rack. Cool for 15 minutes. (If necessary, pour out any rendered fat that has collected below the basket in the machine.)
4. Cut the sausage links in half lengthwise. Sandwich half a string cheese stick between two sausage halves, trimming the ends so the cheese doesn't stick out beyond the meat.
5. Roll each piece of puff pastry into a 6 x 6-inch square on a clean, dry work surface. Set the sausage-cheese sandwich at one edge and roll it up in the dough. The ends will be open like a pig-in-a-blanket. Repeat with the remaining puff pastry, sausage, and cheese.
6. Set the rolls seam side down in the basket. Air-fry undisturbed for 6 minutes, or until puffed and golden brown.
7. Use a nonstick-safe spatula, and perhaps a flatware fork for balance, to transfer the rolls to a wire rack. Cool for at least 5 minutes before serving.

Mediterranean Potato Skins

Servings: 4
Cooking Time: 50 Minutes
Ingredients:

- 2 russet potatoes
- 3 tbsp olive oil
- Salt and pepper to taste
- 2 tbsp rosemary, chopped
- 10 Kalamata olives, diced
- ¼ cup crumbled feta
- 2 tbsp chopped dill

Directions:

1. Preheat air fryer to 380°F. Poke 2-3 holes in the potatoes with a fork. Drizzle them with some olive oil and sprinkle with salt. Put the potatoes into the frying basket and Bake for 30 minutes. When the potatoes are ready, remove them from the fryer and slice in half. Scoop out the flesh of the potatoes with a spoon, leaving a ½-inch layer of potato inside the skins, and set the skins aside.
2. Combine the scooped potato middles with the remaining olive oil, salt, black pepper, and rosemary in a medium bowl. Mix until well combined. Spoon the potato filling into the potato skins, spreading it evenly over them. Top with olives, dill and feta. Put the loaded potato skins back into the air fryer and Bake for 15 minutes. Enjoy!

Crispy Ravioli Bites

Servings: 5
Cooking Time: 7 Minutes
Ingredients:

- ⅓ cup All-purpose flour
- 1 Large egg(s), well beaten
- ⅔ cup Seasoned Italian-style dried bread crumbs
- 10 ounces (about 20) Frozen mini ravioli, meat or cheese, thawed
- Olive oil spray

Directions:

1. Preheat the air fryer to 400°F.
2. Pour the flour into a medium bowl. Set up and fill two shallow soup plates or small pie plates on your counter: one with the beaten egg(s) and one with the bread crumbs.
3. Pour all the ravioli into the flour and toss well to coat. Pick up 1 ravioli, gently shake off any excess flour, and dip the ravioli in the egg(s), coating both sides. Let any excess egg slip back into the rest, then set the ravioli in the bread crumbs, turning it several times until lightly and evenly coated on all sides. Set aside on a cutting board and continue on with the remaining ravioli.
4. Lightly coat the ravioli on both sides with olive oil spray, then set them in the basket in as close to a single layer as you can. Some can lean up against the side of the basket. Air-fry for 7 minutes, tossing the basket at the 4-minute mark to rearrange the pieces, until brown and crisp.
5. Pour the contents of the basket onto a wire rack. Cool for 5 minutes before serving.

Bacon-wrapped Goat Cheese Poppers

Servings: 10

Cooking Time: 10 Minutes

Ingredients:

- 10 large jalapeño peppers
- 8 ounces goat cheese
- 10 slices bacon

Directions:

1. Preheat the air fryer to 380°F.
2. Slice the jalapeños in half. Carefully remove the veins and seeds of the jalapeños with a spoon.
3. Fill each jalapeño half with 2 teaspoons goat cheese.
4. Cut the bacon in half lengthwise to make long strips. Wrap the jalapeños with bacon, trying to cover the entire length of the jalapeño.
5. Place the bacon-wrapped jalapeños into the air fryer basket. Cook the stuffed jalapeños for 10 minutes or until bacon is crispy.

Warm And Salty Edamame

Servings: 4

Cooking Time: 10 Minutes

Ingredients:

- 1 pound Unshelled edamame
- Vegetable oil spray
- ¾ teaspoon Coarse sea salt or kosher salt

Directions:

1. Preheat the air fryer to 400°F.
2. Place the edamame in a large bowl and lightly coat them with vegetable oil spray. Toss well, spray again, and toss until they are evenly coated.
3. When the machine is at temperature, pour the edamame into the basket and air-fry, tossing the basket quite often to rearrange the edamame, for 7 minutes, or until warm and aromatic. (Air-fry for 10 minutes if the edamame were frozen and not thawed.)
4. Pour the edamame into a bowl and sprinkle the salt on top. Toss well, then set aside for a couple of minutes before serving with an empty bowl on the side for the pods.

Cuban Sliders

Servings: 8

Cooking Time: 8 Minutes

Ingredients:

- 8 slices ciabatta bread, ¼-inch thick
- cooking spray
- 1 tablespoon brown mustard
- 6-8 ounces thin sliced leftover roast pork
- 4 ounces thin deli turkey
- ⅓ cup bread and butter pickle slices
- 2–3 ounces Pepper Jack cheese slices

Directions:

1. Spray one side of each slice of bread with butter or olive oil cooking spray.
2. Spread brown mustard on other side of each slice.
3. Layer pork roast, turkey, pickles, and cheese on 4 of the slices. Top with remaining slices.
4. Cook at 390°F for approximately 8minutes. The sandwiches should be golden brown.
5. Cut each slider in half to make 8 portions.

Spanish Fried Baby Squid

Servings: 2

Cooking Time: 30 Minutes

Ingredients:

- 1 cup baby squid
- ½ cup semolina flour
- ½ tsp Spanish paprika
- ½ tsp garlic powder
- 2 eggs
- Salt and pepper to taste
- 2 tbsp lemon juice
- 1 tsp Old Bay seasoning

Directions:

1. Preheat air fryer to 350°F. Beat the eggs in a bowl. Stir in lemon juice and set aside. Mix flour, Old Bay seasoning, garlic powder, paprika, salt, and pepper in another bowl. Dip each piece of squid into the flour, then into the eggs, and then again. Transfer them to the greased frying basket and Air Fry for 18-20 minutes, shaking the basket occasionally until crispy and golden brown. Serve hot.

Easy Crab Cakes

Servings: 4
Cooking Time: 20 Minutes
Ingredients:

- 1 cup lump crab meat
- 2 green onions, minced
- 3 garlic cloves, minced
- ½ lime, juiced
- 2 tbsp mayonnaise
- 2 eggs, beaten
- 1 tsp fresh grated ginger
- ½ tsp allspice
- ½ cup breadcrumbs
- 2 tsp oyster sauce
- 2 tsp spicy mustard
- Pinch of black pepper

Directions:

1. Preheat air fryer to 350°F. Place the crab meat, lime juice, mayonnaise, onions, garlic, ginger, oyster sauce, mustard, allspice, and black pepper in a large mixing bowl. Stir thoroughly until all the ingredients are evenly combined.
2. Form the mixture into patties. Dip the patties into the beaten eggs, and then roll in the breadcrumbs, coating thoroughly on all sides. Place the coated cakes in the lined frying basket and Air Fry for 5 minutes. Flip the cakes over and cook for another 5 minutes until golden brown and crispy on the outside and tantalizingly juicy on the inside. Serve hot.

Spiced Nuts

Servings: 3
Cooking Time: 25 Minutes
Ingredients:

- 1 egg white, lightly beaten
- ¼ cup sugar
- 1 teaspoon salt
- ½ teaspoon ground cinnamon
- ¼ teaspoon ground cloves
- ¼ teaspoon ground allspice
- pinch ground cayenne pepper
- 1 cup pecan halves
- 1 cup cashews
- 1 cup almonds

Directions:

1. Combine the egg white with the sugar and spices in a bowl.
2. Preheat the air fryer to 300°F.
3. Spray or brush the air fryer basket with vegetable oil. Toss the nuts together in the spiced egg white and transfer the nuts to the air fryer basket.
4. Air-fry for 25 minutes, stirring the nuts in the basket a few times during the cooking process. Taste the nuts to see if they are crunchy and nicely toasted. Air-fry for a few more minutes if necessary.
5. Serve warm or cool to room temperature and store in an airtight container for up to two weeks.

Spicy Chicken And Pepper Jack Cheese Bites

Servings: 8
Cooking Time: 8 Minutes
Ingredients:

- 8 ounces cream cheese, softened
- 2 cups grated pepper jack cheese
- 1 Jalapeño pepper, diced
- 2 scallions, minced
- 1 teaspoon paprika
- 2 teaspoons salt, divided
- 3 cups shredded cooked chicken
- ¼ cup all-purpose flour*
- 2 eggs, lightly beaten
- 1 cup panko breadcrumbs*
- olive oil, in a spray bottle
- salsa

Directions:

1. Beat the cream cheese in a bowl until it is smooth and easy to stir. Add the pepper jack cheese, Jalapeño pepper, scallions, paprika and 1 teaspoon of salt. Fold in the shredded cooked chicken and combine well. Roll this mixture into 1-inch balls.
2. Set up a dredging station with three shallow dishes. Place the flour into one shallow dish. Place the eggs into a second shallow dish. Finally, combine the panko breadcrumbs and remaining teaspoon of salt in a third dish.
3. Coat the chicken cheese balls by rolling each ball in the flour first, then dip them into the eggs and finally roll them

in the panko breadcrumbs to coat all sides. Refrigerate for at least 30 minutes.

4. Preheat the air fryer to 400°F.
5. Spray the chicken cheese balls with oil and air-fry in batches for 8 minutes. Shake the basket a few times throughout the cooking process to help the balls brown evenly.
6. Serve hot with salsa on the side.

Cheesy Pigs In A Blanket

Servings: 4
Cooking Time: 7 Minutes
Ingredients:

- 24 cocktail size smoked sausages
- 6 slices deli-sliced Cheddar cheese, each cut into 8 rectangular pieces
- 1 (8-ounce) tube refrigerated crescent roll dough
- ketchup or mustard for dipping

Directions:

1. Unroll the crescent roll dough into one large sheet. If your crescent roll dough has perforated seams, pinch or roll all the perforated seams together. Cut the large sheet of dough into 4 rectangles. Then cut each rectangle into 6 pieces by making one slice lengthwise in the middle and 2 slices horizontally. You should have 24 pieces of dough.
2. Make a deep slit lengthwise down the center of the cocktail sausage. Stuff two pieces of cheese into the slit in the sausage. Roll one piece of crescent dough around the stuffed cocktail sausage leaving the ends of the sausage exposed. Pinch the seam together. Repeat with the remaining sausages.
3. Preheat the air fryer to 350°F.
4. Air-fry in 2 batches, placing the sausages seam side down in the basket. Air-fry for 7 minutes. Serve hot with ketchup or your favorite mustard for dipping.

Rich Clam Spread

Servings: 6
Cooking Time: 40 Minutes
Ingredients:

- 2 cans chopped clams in clam juice
- 1/3 cup panko bread crumbs
- 1 garlic clove, minced
- 1 tbsp olive oil
- 1 tbsp lemon juice
- ¼ tsp hot sauce
- 1 tsp Worcestershire sauce
- ½ tsp shallot powder
- ¼ tsp dried dill
- Salt and pepper to taste
- ½ tsp sweet paprika
- 4 tsp grated Parmesan cheese
- 2 celery stalks, chopped

Directions:

1. Completely drain one can of clams. Add them to a bowl along with the entire can of clams, breadcrumbs, garlic, olive oil, lemon juice, Worcestershire sauce, hot sauce, shallot powder, dill, pepper, salt, paprika, and 2 tbsp Parmesan. Combine well and set aside for 10 minutes. After that time, put the mixture in a greased baking dish.
2. Preheat air fryer to 325°F. Put the dish in the air fryer and Bake for 10 minutes. Sprinkle the remaining paprika and Parmesan, and continue to cook until golden brown on top, 8-10 minutes. Serve hot along with celery sticks.

Olive & Pepper Tapenade

Servings: 4
Cooking Time: 10 Minutes
Ingredients:

- 1 red bell pepper
- 3 tbsp olive oil
- ½ cup black olives, chopped
- 1 garlic clove, minced
- ½ tsp dried oregano
- 1 tbsp white wine juice

Directions:

1. Preheat air fryer to 380°F. Lightly brush the outside of the bell pepper with some olive oil and put it in the frying basket. Roast for 5 minutes. Combine the remaining olive oil with olives, garlic, oregano, and white wine in a bowl. Remove the red pepper from the air fryer, then gently slice off the stem and discard the seeds. Chop into small pieces. Add the chopped pepper to the olive mixture and stir all together until combined. Serve and enjoy!

Cheese Straws

Servings: 8
Cooking Time: 7 Minutes
Ingredients:

- For dusting All-purpose flour
- Two quarters of one thawed sheet (that is, a half of the sheet cut into two even pieces; wrap and refreeze the remainder) A 17.25-ounce box frozen puff pastry
- 1 Large egg(s)
- 2 tablespoons Water
- ¼ cup (about ¾ ounce) Finely grated Parmesan cheese
- up to 1 teaspoon Ground black pepper

Directions:

1. Preheat the air fryer to 400°F.
2. Dust a clean, dry work surface with flour. Set one of the pieces of puff pastry on top, dust the pastry lightly with flour, and roll with a rolling pin to a 6-inch square.
3. Whisk the egg(s) and water in a small or medium bowl until uniform. Brush the pastry square(s) generously with this mixture. Sprinkle each square with 2 tablespoons grated cheese and up to ½ teaspoon ground black pepper.
4. Cut each square into 4 even strips. Grasp each end of 1 strip with clean, dry hands; twist it into a cheese straw. Place the twisted straws on a baking sheet.
5. Lay as many straws as will fit in the air-fryer basket—as a general rule, 4 of them in a small machine, 5 in a medium model, or 6 in a large. There should be space for air to circulate around the straws. Set the baking sheet with any remaining straws in the fridge.
6. Air-fry undisturbed for 7 minutes, or until puffed and crisp. Use tongs to transfer the cheese straws to a wire rack, then make subsequent batches in the same way (keeping the baking sheet with the remaining straws in the fridge as each batch cooks). Serve warm.

Marmalade-almond Topped Brie

Servings:6
Cooking Time: 35 Minutes
Ingredients:

- 1 cup almonds
- 1 egg white, beaten
- ⅛ tsp ground cumin
- ⅛ tsp cayenne pepper
- 1 tsp ground cinnamon
- ¼ tsp powdered sugar
- 1 round Brie cheese
- 2 tbsp orange marmalade

Directions:

1. Preheat air fryer to 325ºF. In a bowl, mix the beaten egg white and almonds. In another bowl, mix the spices and sugar. Stir in almonds, drained of excess egg white. Transfer the almonds to the frying basket and Bake for 12 minutes, tossing once. Let cool for 5 minutes. When cooled, chop into smaller bits. Adjust the air fryer temperature to 400°F. Place the Brie on a parchment-lined pizza pan and Bake for 10 minutes. Transfer the Brie to a serving plate, spread orange marmalade on top, and garnish with spiced walnuts. Serve and enjoy!

Avocado Egg Rolls

Servings: 8
Cooking Time: 8 Minutes
Ingredients:

- 8 full-size egg roll wrappers
- 1 medium avocado, sliced into 8 pieces
- 1 cup cooked black beans, divided
- ½ cup mild salsa, divided
- ½ cup shredded Mexican cheese, divided
- ⅓ cup filtered water, divided
- ½ cup sour cream
- 1 teaspoon chipotle hot sauce

Directions:

1. Preheat the air fryer to 400°F.
2. Place the egg roll wrapper on a flat surface and place 1 strip of avocado down in the center.
3. Top the avocado with 2 tablespoons of black beans, 1 tablespoon of salsa, and 1 tablespoon of shredded cheese.
4. Place two of your fingers into the water, and then moisten the four outside edges of the egg roll wrapper with water (so the outer edges will secure shut).
5. Fold the bottom corner up, covering the filling. Then secure the sides over the top, remembering to lightly moisten them so they stick. Tightly roll the egg roll up and moisten the final flap of the wrapper and firmly press it into the egg roll to secure it shut.
6. Repeat Steps 2–5 until all 8 egg rolls are complete.

7. When ready to cook, spray the air fryer basket with olive oil spray and place the egg rolls into the basket. Depending on the size and type of air fryer you have, you may need to do this in two sets.
8. Cook for 4 minutes, flip, and then cook the remaining 4 minutes.
9. Repeat until all the egg rolls are cooked. Meanwhile, mix the sour cream with the hot sauce to serve as a dipping sauce.
10. Serve warm.

Chicken Nachos

Servings: 6
Cooking Time: 25 Minutes
Ingredients:

- 2 oz baked corn tortilla chips
- 1 cup leftover roast chicken, shredded
- ½ cup canned black beans
- 1 red bell pepper, chopped
- ½ grated carrot
- 1 jalapeño pepper, minced
- 1/3 cup grated Swiss cheese
- 1 tomato, chopped

Directions:

1. Preheat air fryer to 360°F. Lay the tortilla chips in a single layer in a baking pan. Add the chicken, black beans, red bell pepper, carrot, jalapeño, and cheese on top. Bake in the air fryer for 9-12 minutes. Make sure the cheese melts and is slightly browned. Serve garnished with tomatoes.

Tomato & Basil Bruschetta

Servings: 4
Cooking Time: 15 Minutes
Ingredients:

- 3 red tomatoes, diced
- ½ ciabatta loaf
- 1 garlic clove, minced
- 1 fresh mozzarella ball, sliced
- 1 tbsp olive oil
- 10 fresh basil, chopped
- 1 tsp balsamic vinegar
- Pinch of salt

Directions:

1. Preheat air fryer to 370°F.Mix tomatoes, olive oil, salt, vinegar, basil, and garlic in a bowl until well combined. Cut the loaf into 6 slices, about 1-inch thick. Spoon the tomato mixture over the bread and top with one mozzarella slice. Repeat for all bruschettas. Put the bruschettas in the foil-lined frying basket and Bake for 5 minutes until golden. Serve.

Roasted Red Pepper Dip

Servings: 2
Cooking Time: 15 Minutes
Ingredients:

- 2 Medium-size red bell pepper(s)
- 1¾ cups (one 15-ounce can) Canned white beans, drained and rinsed
- 1 tablespoon Fresh oregano leaves, packed
- 3 tablespoons Olive oil
- 1 tablespoon Lemon juice
- ½ teaspoon Table salt
- ½ teaspoon Ground black pepper

Directions:

1. Preheat the air fryer to 400°F.
2. Set the pepper(s) in the basket and air-fry undisturbed for 15 minutes, until blistered and even blackened.
3. Use kitchen tongs to transfer the pepper(s) to a zip-closed plastic bag or small bowl. Seal the bag or cover the bowl with plastic wrap. Set aside for 20 minutes.
4. Peel each pepper, then stem it, cut it in half, and remove all its seeds and their white membranes.
5. Set the pieces of the pepper in a food processor. Add the beans, oregano, olive oil, lemon juice, salt, and pepper. Cover and process until smooth, stopping the machine at least once to scrape down the inside of the canister. Scrape the dip into a bowl and serve warm, or cover and refrigerate for up to 3 days (although the dip tastes best if it's allowed to come back to room temperature).

Apple Rollups

Servings: 8
Cooking Time: 5 Minutes
Ingredients:

- 8 slices whole wheat sandwich bread
- 4 ounces Colby Jack cheese, grated
- ½ small apple, chopped
- 2 tablespoons butter, melted

Directions:

1. Remove crusts from bread and flatten the slices with rolling pin. Don't be gentle. Press hard so that bread will be very thin.
2. Top bread slices with cheese and chopped apple, dividing the ingredients evenly.
3. Roll up each slice tightly and secure each with one or two toothpicks.
4. Brush outside of rolls with melted butter.
5. Place in air fryer basket and cook at 390°F for 5minutes, until outside is crisp and nicely browned.

Fried Olives

Servings: 5
Cooking Time: 10 Minutes
Ingredients:

- ⅓ cup All-purpose flour or tapioca flour
- 1 Large egg white(s)
- 1 tablespoon Brine from the olive jar
- ⅔ cup Plain dried bread crumbs (gluten-free, if a concern)
- 15 Large pimiento-stuffed green olives
- Olive oil spray

Directions:

1. Preheat the air fryer to 400°F.
2. Pour the flour in a medium-size zip-closed plastic bag. Whisk the egg white and pickle brine in a medium bowl until foamy. Spread out the bread crumbs on a dinner plate.
3. Pour all the olives into the bag with the flour, seal, and shake to coat the olives. Remove a couple of olives, shake off any excess flour, and drop them into the egg white mixture. Toss gently but well to coat. Pick them up one at a time and roll each in the bread crumbs until well coated on all sides, even the ends. Set them aside on a cutting board as you finish the rest. When done, coat the olives with olive oil spray on all sides.
4. Place the olives in the basket in one layer. Air-fry for 8 minutes, gently shaking the basket once halfway through the cooking process to rearrange the olives, until lightly browned.
5. Gently pour the olives onto a wire rack and cool for at least 10 minutes before serving. Once cooled, the olives may be stored in a sealed container in the fridge for up to 2 days. To rewarm them, set them in the basket of a heated 400°F air fryer undisturbed for 2 minutes.

Korean Brussels Sprouts

Servings: 4
Cooking Time: 20 Minutes
Ingredients:

- 1 lb Brussels sprouts
- 1 ½ tbsp maple syrup
- 1 ½ tsp white miso
- 1 tsp toasted sesame oil
- 1 ½ tsp soy sauce
- 2 garlic cloves, minced
- 1 tsp grated fresh ginger
- ½ tsp Gochugaru chili flakes

Directions:

1. Preheat air fryer to 390°F. Place the Brussels sprouts in the greased basket, spray with oil and Air Fry for 10-14 minutes, tossing once until crispy, tender, and golden.
2. In a bowl, combine maple syrup and miso. Whisk until smooth. Add the sesame oil, soy sauce, garlic, ginger, and Gochugaru flakes. Stir well. When the Brussels sprouts are done, add them to the bowl and toss with the sauce. Serve immediately.

Fried Cheese Ravioli With Marinara Sauce

Servings: 4
Cooking Time: 7 Minutes
Ingredients:

- 1 pound cheese ravioli, fresh or frozen
- 2 eggs, lightly beaten
- 1 cup plain breadcrumbs
- ½ teaspoon paprika
- ½ teaspoon dried oregano
- ½ teaspoon salt
- grated Parmesan cheese
- chopped fresh parsley
- 1 to 2 cups marinara sauce (jarred or homemade)

Directions:

1. Bring a stockpot of salted water to a boil. Boil the ravioli according to the package directions and then drain. Let the cooked ravioli cool to a temperature where you can comfortably handle them.
2. While the pasta is cooking, set up a dredging station with two shallow dishes. Place the eggs into one dish. Combine the breadcrumbs, paprika, dried oregano and salt in the other dish.
3. Preheat the air fryer to 380°F.
4. Working with one at a time, dip the cooked ravioli into the egg, coating all sides. Then press the ravioli into the breadcrumbs, making sure that all sides are covered. Transfer the ravioli to the air fryer basket, cooking in batches, one layer at a time. Air-fry at 380°F for 7 minutes.
5. While the ravioli is air-frying, bring the marinara sauce to a simmer on the stovetop. Transfer to a small bowl.
6. Sprinkle a little Parmesan cheese and chopped parsley on top of the fried ravioli and serve warm with the marinara sauce on the side for dipping.

Potato Chips With Sour Cream And Onion Dip

Servings: 2
Cooking Time: 20 Minutes
Ingredients:

- 2 large potatoes (Yukon Gold or russet)
- vegetable or olive oil in a spray bottle
- sea salt and freshly ground black pepper
- Sour Cream and Onion Dip:
- ½ cup sour cream
- 1 tablespoon olive oil
- 2 scallions, white part only minced
- ¼ teaspoon salt
- freshly ground black pepper
- a squeeze of lemon juice (about ¼ teaspoon)

Directions:

1. Wash the potatoes well, but leave the skins on. Slice them into ⅛-inch thin slices, using a mandolin or food processor. Rinse the potatoes under cold water until the water runs clear and then let them soak in a bowl of cold water for at least 10 minutes. Drain and dry the potato slices really well in a single layer on a clean kitchen towel.
2. Preheat the air fryer to 300°F. Spray the potato chips with the oil so that both sides are evenly coated, or rub the slices between your hands with some oil if you don't have a spray bottle.
3. Air-fry in two batches at 300°F for 20 minutes, shaking the basket a few times during the cooking process so the chips crisp and brown more evenly. Season the finished chips with sea salt and freshly ground black pepper while they are still hot.
4. While the chips are air-frying, make the sour cream and onion dip by mixing together the sour cream, olive oil, scallions, salt, pepper and lemon juice. Serve the chips warm or at room temperature along with the dip.

Potato Samosas

Servings: 12
Cooking Time: 10 Minutes
Ingredients:

- ¾ cup Instant mashed potato flakes
- ¾ cup Boiling water
- ⅓ cup Plain full-fat or low-fat yogurt (not Greek yogurt or fat-free yogurt)
- 1 teaspoon Yellow curry powder, purchased or homemade (see here)
- ½ teaspoon Table salt
- 1½ Purchased refrigerated pie crust(s), from a minimum 14.1-ounce box
- All-purpose flour
- Vegetable oil spray

Directions:

1. Put the potato flakes in a medium bowl and pour the boiling water over them. Stir well to form a mixture like thick mashed potatoes. Cool for 15 minutes.
2. Preheat the air fryer to 400°F.
3. Stir the yogurt, curry powder, and salt into the potato mixture until smooth and uniform.
4. Unwrap and unroll the sheet(s) of pie crust dough onto a clean, dry work surface. Cut out as many 4-inch circles as you can with a big cookie cutter or a giant sturdy water glass, or even by tracing the circle with the rim of a 4-inch plate. Gather up the scraps of dough. Lightly flour your work surface and set the scraps on top. Roll them together into a sheet that matches the thickness of the original crusts and cut more circles until you have the number you need—8 circles for the small batch, 12 for the medium batch, or 16 for the large.
5. Pick up one of the circles and create something like an ice cream cone by folding and sealing the circle together so that it is closed at the bottom and flared open at the top, in a conical shape. Put 1 tablespoon of the potato filling into the open cone, then push the filling into the cone toward the point. Fold the top over the filling and press to seal the dough into a triangular shape with corners, taking care to seal those corners all around. Set aside and continue forming and filling the remainder of the dough circles as directed.
6. Lightly coat the filled dough pockets with vegetable oil spray on all sides. Set them in the basket in one layer and air-fry undisturbed for 10 minutes, or until lightly browned and crisp.
7. Gently turn the contents of the basket out onto a wire rack. Use kitchen tongs to gently set all the samosas seam side up. Cool for 10 minutes before serving.

Home-style Reuben Spread

Servings:6

Cooking Time: 20 Minutes

Ingredients:

- 8 oz cream cheese, softened
- 1 cup chopped deli corned beef
- ¼ cup mayonnaise
- ¼ cup sour cream
- 1 cup drained sauerkraut
- 1 cup grated Gruyère cheese
- 1 tsp caraway seeds
- 2 tbsp parsley, chopped

Directions:

1. Preheat air fryer to 400ºF. Add the cream cheese, mayo, and sour cream in a bowl and stir until combined. Add corned beef, sauerkraut, ½ cup of Gruyere cheese, parsley and caraway seeds. Spoon the mixture into a baking dish and top with the remaining cheese Place the dish in the frying basket and Bake for 10 minutes. Serve.

Beet Chips With Guacamole

Servings: 4

Cooking Time: 40 Minutes

Ingredients:

- 2 avocados, cubed
- 2 tbsp lime juice
- Celery salt to taste
- 2 beets, peeled
- 2 eggs, beaten
- 1 cup panko bread crumbs
- ½ tsp paprika

Directions:

1. Preheat the air fryer to 375°F. Mash the avocados, lime juice, and celery salt in a bowl, then pour the guacamole into a serving bowl, cover, and refrigerate. Slice the beets into 3-inch long sticks that are ½ inch thick. Beat the eggs in a shallow bowl and combine the panko and paprika on a plate. Dip the fries in the egg, then the panko mixture, coating well. Put the beets in the frying basket and spray with cooking oil, then Air Fry for 18-22 minutes or until crispy and golden. Serve with guacamole.

Stuffed Mushrooms

Servings: 10

Cooking Time: 8 Minutes

Ingredients:

- 8 ounces white mushroom caps, stems removed
- salt
- 6 fresh mozzarella cheese balls
- ground dried thyme
- ¼ roasted red pepper cut into small pieces (about ½ inch)

Directions:

1. Sprinkle inside of mushroom caps with salt to taste.
2. Cut mozzarella balls in half.
3. Stuff each cap with half a mozzarella cheese ball. Sprinkle very lightly with thyme.
4. Top each mushroom with a small strip of roasted red pepper, lightly pressing it into the cheese.
5. Cook at 390°F for 8minutes or longer if you prefer softer mushrooms.

Poultry Recipes

Sweet Chili Spiced Chicken

Servings: 4

Cooking Time: 43 Minutes

Ingredients:

- Spice Rub:
- 2 tablespoons brown sugar
- 2 tablespoons paprika
- 1 teaspoon dry mustard powder
- 1 teaspoon chili powder
- 2 tablespoons coarse sea salt or kosher salt
- 2 teaspoons coarsely ground black pepper
- 1 tablespoon vegetable oil
- 1 (3½-pound) chicken, cut into 8 pieces

Directions:

1. Prepare the spice rub by combining the brown sugar, paprika, mustard powder, chili powder, salt and pepper. Rub the oil all over the chicken pieces and then rub the spice mix onto the chicken, covering completely. This is done very easily in a zipper sealable bag. You can do this ahead of time and let the chicken marinate in the refrigerator, or just proceed with cooking right away.
2. Preheat the air fryer to 370°F.
3. Air-fry the chicken in two batches. Place the two chicken thighs and two drumsticks into the air fryer basket. Air-fry at 370°F for 10 minutes. Then, gently turn the chicken pieces over and air-fry for another 10 minutes. Remove the chicken pieces and let them rest on a plate while you cook the chicken breasts. Air-fry the chicken breasts, skin side down for 8 minutes. Turn the chicken breasts over and air-fry for another 12 minutes.
4. Lower the temperature of the air fryer to 340°F. Place the first batch of chicken on top of the second batch already in the basket and air-fry for a final 3 minutes.
5. Let the chicken rest for 5 minutes and serve warm with some mashed potatoes and a green salad or vegetables.

Berry-glazed Turkey Breast

Servings: 4

Cooking Time: 1 Hour 25 Minutes

Ingredients:

- 1 bone-in, skin-on turkey breast
- 1 tbsp olive oil
- Salt and pepper to taste
- 1 cup raspberries
- 1cup chopped strawberries
- 2 tbsp balsamic vinegar
- 2 tbsp butter, melted
- 1 tbsp honey mustard
- 1 tsp dried rosemary

Directions:

1. Preheat the air fryer to 350°F. Lay the turkey breast skin-side up in the frying basket, brush with the oil, and sprinkle with salt and pepper. Bake for 55-65 minutes, flipping twice. Meanwhile, mix the berries, vinegar, melted butter, rosemary and honey mustard in a blender and blend until smooth. Turn the turkey skin-side up inside the fryer and brush with half of the berry mix. Bake for 5 more minutes. Put the remaining berry mix in a small saucepan and simmer for 3-4 minutes while the turkey cooks. When the turkey is done, let it stand for 10 minutes, then carve. Serve with the remaining glaze.

Chicken Strips

Servings: 4

Cooking Time: 8 Minutes

Ingredients:

- 1 pound chicken tenders
- Marinade
- ¼ cup olive oil
- 2 tablespoons water
- 2 tablespoons honey
- 2 tablespoons white vinegar
- ½ teaspoon salt
- ½ teaspoon crushed red pepper
- 1 teaspoon garlic powder
- 1 teaspoon onion powder
- ½ teaspoon paprika

Directions:

1. Combine all marinade ingredients and mix well.
2. Add chicken and stir to coat. Cover tightly and let marinate in refrigerator for 30minutes.
3. Remove tenders from marinade and place them in a single layer in the air fryer basket.
4. Cook at 390°F for 3minutes. Turn tenders over and cook for 5 minutes longer or until chicken is done and juices run clear.
5. Repeat step 4 to cook remaining tenders.

Parmesan Crusted Chicken Cordon Bleu

Servings: 2

Cooking Time: 14 Minutes

Ingredients:

- 2 (6-ounce) boneless, skinless chicken breasts
- salt and freshly ground black pepper
- 1 tablespoon Dijon mustard
- 4 slices Swiss cheese
- 4 slices deli-sliced ham
- ¼ cup all-purpose flour*
- 1 egg, beaten
- ¾ cup panko breadcrumbs*
- ⅓ cup grated Parmesan cheese
- olive oil, in a spray bottle

Directions:

1. Butterfly the chicken breasts. Place the chicken breast on a cutting board and press down on the breast with the palm of your hand. Slice into the long side of the chicken breast, parallel to the cutting board, but not all the way through to the other side. Open the chicken breast like a "book". Place a piece of plastic wrap over the chicken breast and gently pound it with a meat mallet to make it evenly thick.
2. Season the chicken with salt and pepper. Spread the Dijon mustard on the inside of each chicken breast. Layer one slice of cheese on top of the mustard, then top with the 2 slices of ham and the other slice of cheese.
3. Starting with the long edge of the chicken breast, roll the chicken up to the other side. Secure it shut with 1 or 2 toothpicks.
4. Preheat the air fryer to 350°F.
5. Set up a dredging station with three shallow dishes. Place the flour in the first dish. Place the beaten egg in the second shallow dish. Combine the panko breadcrumbs and Parmesan cheese together in the third shallow dish. Dip the stuffed and rolled chicken breasts in the flour, then the beaten egg and then roll in the breadcrumb-cheese mixture to cover on all sides. Press the crumbs onto the chicken breasts with your hands to make sure they are well adhered. Spray the chicken breasts with olive oil and transfer to the air fryer basket.
6. Air-fry at 350°F for 14 minutes, flipping the breasts over halfway through the cooking time. Let the chicken rest for a few minutes before removing the toothpicks, slicing and serving.

Chicago-style Turkey Meatballs

Servings: 6
Cooking Time: 15 Minutes
Ingredients:

- 1 lb ground turkey
- 1 tbsp orange juice
- Salt and pepper to taste
- ½ tsp smoked paprika
- ½ tsp chili powder
- 1 tsp cumin powder
- ¼ red bell pepper, diced
- 1 diced jalapeño pepper
- 2 garlic cloves, minced

Directions:

1. Preheat air fryer to 400°F. Combine all of the ingredients in a large bowl. Shape into meatballs. Transfer the meatballs into the greased frying basket. Air Fry for 4 minutes, then flip the meatballs. Air Fry for another 3 minutes until cooked through. Serve immediately.

Gingery Turkey Meatballs

Servings: 4
Cooking Time: 25 Minutes
Ingredients:

- ¼ cup water chestnuts, chopped
- ¼ cup panko bread crumbs
- 1 lb ground turkey
- ½ tsp ground ginger
- 2 tbsp fish sauce
- 1 tbsp sesame oil
- 1 small onion, minced
- 1 egg, beaten

Directions:

1. Preheat air fryer to 400°F. Place the ground turkey, water chestnuts, ground ginger, fish sauce, onion, egg, and bread crumbs in a bowl and stir to combine. Form the turkey mixture into 1-inch meatballs. Arrange the meatballs in the baking pan. Drizzle with sesame oil. Bake until the meatballs are cooked through, 10-12 minutes, flipping once. Serve and enjoy!

Gruyère Asparagus & Chicken Quiche

Servings: 4
Cooking Time: 30 Minutes
Ingredients:

- 1 grilled chicken breasts, diced
- ½ cup shredded Gruyère cheese
- 1 premade pie crust
- 2 eggs, beaten
- ¼ cup milk
- Salt and pepper to taste
- ½ lb asparagus, sliced
- 1 lemon, zested

Directions:

1. Preheat air fryer to 360°F.Carefully press the crust into a baking dish, trimming the edges. Prick the dough with a fork a few times. Add the eggs, milk, asparagus, salt, pepper, chicken, lemon zest, and half of Gruyère cheese to a mixing bowl and stir until completely blended. Pour the mixture into the pie crust. Bake in the air fryer for 15 minutes. Sprinkle the remaining Gruyère cheese on top of the quiche filling. Bake for 5 more minutes until the quiche is golden brown. Remove and allow to cool for a few minutes before cutting. Serve sliced and enjoy!

Restaurant-style Chicken Thighs

Servings: 4
Cooking Time: 30 Minutes
Ingredients:

- 1 lb boneless, skinless chicken thighs
- ¼ cup barbecue sauce
- 2 cloves garlic, minced
- 1 tsp lemon zest
- 2 tbsp parsley, chopped
- 2 tbsp lemon juice

Directions:

1. Coat the chicken with barbecue sauce, garlic, and lemon juice in a medium bowl. leave to marinate for 10 minutes.
2. Preheat air fryer to 380°F. When ready to cook, remove the chicken from the bowl and shake off any drips. Arrange

the chicken in the air fryer and Bake for 16-18 minutes, until golden and cooked through. Serve topped with lemon zest and parsley. Enjoy!

Chicken Meatballs With A Surprise

Servings:4
Cooking Time: 35 Minutes
Ingredients:

- 1/3 cup cottage cheese crumbles
- 1 lb ground chicken
- ½ tsp onion powder
- ¼ cup chopped basil
- ½ cup bread crumbs
- ½ tsp garlic powder

Directions:

1. Preheat air fryer to 350°F. Combine the ground chicken, onion, basil, cottage cheese, bread crumbs, and garlic powder in a bowl. Form into 18 meatballs, about 2 tbsp each. Place the chicken meatballs in the greased frying basket and Air Fry for 12 minutes, shaking once. Serve.

Sticky Drumsticks

Servings: 4
Cooking Time: 45 Minutes
Ingredients:

- 1 lb chicken drumsticks
- 1 tbsp chicken seasoning
- 1 tsp dried chili flakes
- Salt and pepper to taste
- ¼ cup honey
- 1 cup barbecue sauce

Directions:

1. Preheat air fryer to 390°F. Season drumsticks with chicken seasoning, chili flakes, salt, and pepper. Place one batch of drumsticks in the greased frying basket and Air Fry for 18-20 minutes, flipping once until golden.
2. While the chicken is cooking, combine honey and barbecue sauce in a small bowl. Remove the drumsticks to a serving dish. Drizzle honey-barbecue sauce over and serve.

Favourite Fried Chicken Wings

Servings: 4
Cooking Time: 30 Minutes
Ingredients:

- 16 chicken wings
- 1 tsp garlic powder
- ½ tsp paprika
- 1 tsp chicken seasoning
- Black pepper to taste
- ½ cup flour
- ¼ cup sour cream
- 2 tsp red chili flakes

Directions:

1. Preheat air fryer to 400°F. Put the drumettes in a resealable bag along with garlic powder, chicken seasoning, paprika, and pepper. Seal the bag and shake until the chicken is completely coated. Prepare a clean resealable bag and add the flour. Pour sour cream in a large bowl. Dunk the drumettes into the sour cream, then transfer them to the bag of flour. Seal the bag and shake until coated and repeat until all of the wings are coated. Transfer the drumettes to the frying basket. Lightly spray them with cooking oil and Air Fry for 23-25 minutes, shaking the basket a few times until crispy and golden brown. Allow to cool slightly. Sprinkle with red chili flakes and serve.

Chicken Tenders With Basil-strawberry Glaze

Servings:4
Cooking Time: 20 Minutes
Ingredients:

- 1 lb chicken tenderloins
- ¼ cup strawberry preserves
- 3 tbsp chopped basil
- 1 tsp orange juice
- ½ tsp orange zest
- Salt and pepper to taste

Directions:

1. Combine all ingredients, except for 1 tbsp of basil, in a bowl. Marinade in the fridge covered for 30 minutes.

2. Preheat air fryer to 350ºF. Place the chicken tenders in the frying basket and Air Fry for 4-6 minutes. Shake gently the basket and turn over the chicken. Cook for 5 more minutes. Top with the remaining basil to serve.

Cajun Fried Chicken

Servings: 3

Cooking Time: 35 Minutes

Ingredients:

- 1 cup Cajun seasoning
- ½ tsp mango powder
- 6 chicken legs, bone-in

Directions:

1. Preheat air fryer to 360°F. Place half of the Cajun seasoning and 3/4 cup of water in a bowl and mix well to dissolve any lumps. Add the remaining Cajun seasoning and mango powder to a shallow bowl and stir to combine. Dip the chicken in the batter, then coat it in the mango seasoning. Lightly spritz the chicken with cooking spray. Place the chicken in the air fryer and Air Fry for 14-16 minutes, turning once until the chicken is cooked and the coating is brown. Serve and enjoy!

Boss Chicken Cobb Salad

Servings: 2

Cooking Time: 30 Minutes

Ingredients:

- 4 oz cooked bacon, crumbled
- ¼ cup diced peeled red onion
- ½ cup crumbled blue cheese
- 1 egg
- 1 tbsp honey
- 1 tbsp Dijon mustard
- ½ tsp apple cider vinegar
- 2 chicken breasts, cubed
- 3/4 cup bread crumbs
- Salt and pepper to taste
- 3 cups torn iceberg lettuce
- 2 cups baby spinach
- ½ cup ranch dressing
- ½ avocado, diced
- 1 beefsteak tomato, diced
- 1 hard-boiled egg, diced
- 2 tbsp parsley

Directions:

1. Preheat air fryer at 350ºF. Mix the egg, honey, mustard, and vinegar in a bowl. Toss in chicken cubes to coat. Shake off excess marinade of chicken. In another bowl, combine breadcrumbs, salt, and pepper. Dredge chicken cubes in the mixture. Place chicken cubes in the greased frying basket. Air Fry for 8-10 minutes, tossing once. In a salad bowl, combine lettuce, baby spinach, and ranch dressing and toss to coat. Add in the cooked chicken and the remaining ingredients. Serve immediately.

Fiesta Chicken Plate

Servings: 4

Cooking Time: 15 Minutes

Ingredients:

- 1 pound boneless, skinless chicken breasts (2 large breasts)
- 2 tablespoons lime juice
- 1 teaspoon cumin
- ½ teaspoon salt
- ½ cup grated Pepper Jack cheese
- 1 16-ounce can refried beans
- ½ cup salsa
- 2 cups shredded lettuce
- 1 medium tomato, chopped
- 2 avocados, peeled and sliced
- 1 small onion, sliced into thin rings
- sour cream
- tortilla chips (optional)

Directions:

1. Split each chicken breast in half lengthwise.
2. Mix lime juice, cumin, and salt together and brush on all surfaces of chicken breasts.
3. Place in air fryer basket and cook at 390°F for 15 minutes, until well done.
4. Divide the cheese evenly over chicken breasts and cook for an additional minute to melt cheese.
5. While chicken is cooking, heat refried beans on stovetop or in microwave.

6. When ready to serve, divide beans among 4 plates. Place chicken breasts on top of beans and spoon salsa over. Arrange the lettuce, tomatoes, and avocados artfully on each plate and scatter with the onion rings.
7. Pass sour cream at the table and serve with tortilla chips if desired.

Chicken Hand Pies

Servings: 8
Cooking Time: 10 Minutes Per Batch
Ingredients:

- ¾ cup chicken broth
- ¾ cup frozen mixed peas and carrots
- 1 cup cooked chicken, chopped
- 1 tablespoon cornstarch
- 1 tablespoon milk
- salt and pepper
- 1 8-count can organic flaky biscuits
- oil for misting or cooking spray

Directions:

1. In a medium saucepan, bring chicken broth to a boil. Stir in the frozen peas and carrots and cook for 5minutes over medium heat. Stir in chicken.
2. Mix the cornstarch into the milk until it dissolves. Stir it into the simmering chicken broth mixture and cook just until thickened.
3. Remove from heat, add salt and pepper to taste, and let cool slightly.
4. Lay biscuits out on wax paper. Peel each biscuit apart in the middle to make 2 rounds so you have 16 rounds total. Using your hands or a rolling pin, flatten each biscuit round slightly to make it larger and thinner.
5. Divide chicken filling among 8 of the biscuit rounds. Place remaining biscuit rounds on top and press edges all around. Use the tines of a fork to crimp biscuit edges and make sure they are sealed well.
6. Spray both sides lightly with oil or cooking spray.
7. Cook in a single layer, 4 at a time, at 330°F for 10minutes or until biscuit dough is cooked through and golden brown.

Lemon Herb Whole Cornish Hen

Servings: 2
Cooking Time: 50 Minutes
Ingredients:

- 1 Cornish hen
- ¼ cup olive oil
- 2 tbsp lemon juice
- 2 tbsp sage, chopped
- 2 tbsp thyme, chopped
- 4 garlic cloves, chopped
- Salt and pepper to taste
- 1 celery stalk, chopped
- ½ small onion
- ½ lemon, juiced and zested
- 2 tbsp chopped parsley

Directions:

1. Preheat air fryer to 380°F. Whisk the olive oil, lemon juice, sage, thyme, garlic, salt, and pepper in a bowl. Rub the mixture on the tops and sides of the hen. Pour any excess inside the cavity of the bird. Stuff the celery, onion, and lemon juice and zest into the cavity of the hen. Put in the frying basket and Roast for 40-45 minutes. Cut the hen in half and serve garnished with parsley.

Chicken Chunks

Servings: 4
Cooking Time: 10 Minutes
Ingredients:

- 1 pound chicken tenders cut in large chunks, about 1½ inches
- salt and pepper
- ½ cup cornstarch
- 2 eggs, beaten
- 1 cup panko breadcrumbs
- oil for misting or cooking spray

Directions:

1. Season chicken chunks to your liking with salt and pepper.
2. Dip chicken chunks in cornstarch. Then dip in egg and shake off excess. Then roll in panko crumbs to coat well.
3. Spray all sides of chicken chunks with oil or cooking spray.

4. Place chicken in air fryer basket in single layer and cook at 390°F for 5minutes. Spray with oil, turn chunks over, and spray other side.
5. Cook for an additional 5minutes or until chicken juices run clear and outside is golden brown.
6. Repeat steps 4 and 5 to cook remaining chicken.

Lemon Sage Roast Chicken

Servings: 4
Cooking Time: 60 Minutes
Ingredients:

- 1 (4-pound) chicken
- 1 bunch sage, divided
- 1 lemon, zest and juice
- salt and freshly ground black pepper

Directions:

1. Preheat the air fryer to 350°F and pour a little water into the bottom of the air fryer drawer. (This will help prevent the grease that drips into the bottom drawer from burning and smoking.)
2. Run your fingers between the skin and flesh of the chicken breasts and thighs. Push a couple of sage leaves up underneath the skin of the chicken on each breast and each thigh.
3. Push some of the lemon zest up under the skin of the chicken next to the sage. Sprinkle some of the zest inside the chicken cavity, and reserve any leftover zest. Squeeze the lemon juice all over the chicken and in the cavity as well.
4. Season the chicken, inside and out, with the salt and freshly ground black pepper. Set a few sage leaves aside for the final garnish. Crumple up the remaining sage leaves and push them into the cavity of the chicken, along with one of the squeezed lemon halves.
5. Place the chicken breast side up into the air fryer basket and air-fry for 20 minutes at 350°F. Flip the chicken over so that it is breast side down and continue to air-fry for another 20 minutes. Return the chicken to breast side up and finish air-frying for 20 more minutes. The internal temperature of the chicken should register 165°F in the thickest part of the thigh when fully cooked. Remove the chicken from the air fryer and let it rest on a cutting board for at least 5 minutes.
6. Cut the rested chicken into pieces, sprinkle with the reserved lemon zest and garnish with the reserved sage leaves.

Chicken Salad With Roasted Vegetables

Servings: 4
Cooking Time: 25 Minutes
Ingredients:

- 4 tbsp honey-mustard salad dressing
- 3 chicken breasts, cubed
- 1 red onion, sliced
- 1 orange bell pepper, sliced
- 1 cup sliced zucchini
- ½ tsp dried thyme
- ½ cup mayonnaise
- 2 tbsp lemon juice

Directions:

1. Preheat air fryer to 400°F. Add chicken, onion, pepper, and zucchini to the fryer. Drizzle with 1 tbsp of the salad dressing and sprinkle with thyme. Toss to coat. Bake for 5-6 minutes. Shake the basket, then continue cooking for another 5-6 minutes. In a bowl, combine the rest of the dressing, mayonnaise, and lemon juice. Transfer the chicken and vegetables and toss to coat. Serve and enjoy!

Mumbai Chicken Nuggets

Servings: 4
Cooking Time: 30 Minutes
Ingredients:

- 1 lb boneless, skinless chicken breasts
- 4 tsp curry powder
- Salt and pepper to taste
- 1 egg, beaten
- 2 tbsp sesame oil
- 1 cup panko bread crumbs
- ½ cup coconut yogurt
- 1/3 cup mango chutney
- ¼ cup mayonnaise

Directions:

1. Preheat the air fryer to 400°F. Cube the chicken into 1-inch pieces and sprinkle with 3 tsp of curry powder, salt, and pepper; toss to coat. Beat together the egg and sesame oil in a shallow bowl and scatter the panko onto a separate plate.

Dip the chicken in the egg, then in the panko, and press to coat. Lay the coated nuggets on a wire rack as you work. Set the nuggets in the greased frying basket and Air Fry for 7-10 minutes, rearranging once halfway through cooking. While the nuggets are cooking, combine the yogurt, chutney, mayonnaise, and the remaining teaspoon of curry powder in a small bowl. Serve the nuggets with the dipping sauce.

Peachy Chicken Chunks With Cherries

Servings: 4
Cooking Time: 16 Minutes
Ingredients:

- ⅓ cup peach preserves
- 1 teaspoon ground rosemary
- ½ teaspoon black pepper
- ½ teaspoon salt
- ½ teaspoon marjoram
- 1 teaspoon light olive oil
- 1 pound boneless chicken breasts, cut in 1½-inch chunks
- oil for misting or cooking spray
- 10-ounce package frozen unsweetened dark cherries, thawed and drained

Directions:
1. In a medium bowl, mix together peach preserves, rosemary, pepper, salt, marjoram, and olive oil.
2. Stir in chicken chunks and toss to coat well with the preserve mixture.
3. Spray air fryer basket with oil or cooking spray and lay chicken chunks in basket.
4. Cook at 390°F for 7minutes. Stir. Cook for 8 more minutes or until chicken juices run clear.
5. When chicken has cooked through, scatter the cherries over and cook for additional minute to heat cherries.

Chilean-style Chicken Empanadas

Servings: 4
Cooking Time: 25 Minutes
Ingredients:

- 4 oz chorizo sausage, casings removed and crumbled
- 1 tbsp olive oil
- 4 oz chicken breasts, diced
- ¼ cup black olives, sliced
- 1 tsp chili powder
- 1 tsp paprika
- ¼ cup raisins
- 4 empanada shells

Directions:
1. Preheat air fryer to 350°F. Warm the oil in a skillet over medium heat. Sauté the chicken and chorizo, breaking up the chorizo, 3-4 minutes. Add the raisins, chili powder, paprika, and olives and stir. Kill the heat and let the mixture cool slightly. Divide the chorizo mixture between the empanada shells and fold them over to cover the filling. Seal edges with water and press down with a fork to secure. Place the empanadas in the frying basket. Bake for 15 minutes, flipping once until golden. Serve warm.

Irresistible Cheesy Chicken Sticks

Servings: 2
Cooking Time: 30 Minutes
Ingredients:

- 6 mozzarella sticks
- 1 cup flour
- 2 eggs, beaten
- 1 lb ground chicken
- 1 ½ cups breadcrumbs
- ¼ tsp crushed chilis
- ¼ tsp cayenne pepper
- ½ tsp garlic powder
- ¼ tsp shallot powder
- ½ tsp oregano

Directions:
1. Preheat air fryer to 390°F. Combine crushed chilis, cayenne pepper, garlic powder, shallot powder, and oregano in a bowl. Add the ground chicken and mix well with your hands until evenly combined. In another mixing bowl, beat the eggs until fluffy and until the yolks and whites are fully combined, and set aside.
2. Pour the beaten eggs, flour, and bread crumbs into 3 separate bowls. Roll the mozzarella sticks in the flour, then dip them in the beaten eggs. With hands, wrap the stick in a

thin layer of the chicken mixture. Finally, coat the sticks in the crumbs. Place the sticks in the greased frying basket fryer and Air Fry for 18-20 minutes, turning once until crispy. Serve hot.

Spring Chicken Salad

Servings: 4
Cooking Time: 25 Minutes
Ingredients:

- 3 chicken breasts, cubed
- 1 small red onion, sliced
- 1 red bell pepper, sliced
- 1 cup green beans, sliced
- 2 tbsp ranch salad dressing
- 2 tbsp lemon juice
- ½ tsp dried basil
- 10 oz spring mix

Directions:

1. Preheat air fryer to 400°F. Put the chicken, red onion, red bell pepper, and green beans in the frying basket and Roast for 10-13 minutes until the chicken is cooked through. Shake the basket at least once while cooking. As the chicken is cooking, combine the ranch dressing, lemon juice, and basil. When the chicken is done, remove it and along with the veggies to a bowl and pour the dressing over. Stir to coat. Serve with spring mix.

Prosciutto Chicken Rolls

Servings: 4
Cooking Time: 30 Minutes
Ingredients:

- ½ cup chopped broccoli
- ½ cup grated cheddar
- 2 scallions, sliced
- 2 garlic cloves, minced
- 4 prosciutto thin slices
- ¼ cup cream cheese
- Salt and pepper to taste
- ½ tsp dried oregano
- ½ tsp dried basil
- 4 chicken breasts
- 2 tbsp chopped cilantro

Directions:

1. Preheat air fryer to 375°F. Combine broccoli, scallion, garlic, Cheddar, cream cheese, salt, pepper, oregano, and basil in a small bowl. Prepare the chicken by placing it between two pieces of plastic wrap. Pound the chicken with a meat mallet or heavy can until it is evenly ½-inch thickness. Top each with a slice of prosciutto and spoon ¼ of the cheese mixture in the center of the chicken breast. Fold each breast over the filling and transfer to a greased baking dish. Place the dish in the frying basket and bake for 8 minutes. Flip the chicken and bake for another 8-12 minutes. Allow resting for 5 minutes. Serve warm sprinkled with cilantro and enjoy!

Spinach & Turkey Meatballs

Servings: 4
Cooking Time: 45 Minutes
Ingredients:

- ¼ cup grated Parmesan cheese
- 2 scallions, chopped
- 1 garlic clove, minced
- 1 egg, beaten
- 1 cup baby spinach
- ¼ cup bread crumbs
- 1 tsp dried oregano
- Salt and pepper to taste
- 1 ¼ lb ground turkey

Directions:

1. Preheat the air fryer to 400°F and preheat the oven to 250°F. Combine the scallions, garlic, egg, baby spinach, breadcrumbs, Parmesan, oregano, salt, and pepper in a bowl and mix well. Add the turkey and mix, then form into 1½-inch balls. Add as many meatballs as will fit in a single layer in the frying basket and Air Fry for 10-15 minutes, shaking once around minute 7. Put the cooked meatballs on a tray in the oven and cover with foil to keep warm. Repeat with the remaining balls.

Spicy Black Bean Turkey Burgers With Cumin-avocado Spread

Servings: 2

Cooking Time: 20 Minutes

Ingredients:

- 1 cup canned black beans, drained and rinsed
- ¾ pound lean ground turkey
- 2 tablespoons minced red onion
- 1 Jalapeño pepper, seeded and minced
- 2 tablespoons plain breadcrumbs
- ½ teaspoon chili powder
- ¼ teaspoon cayenne pepper
- salt, to taste
- olive or vegetable oil
- 2 slices pepper jack cheese
- toasted burger rolls, sliced tomatoes, lettuce leaves
- Cumin-Avocado Spread:
- 1 ripe avocado
- juice of 1 lime
- 1 teaspoon ground cumin
- ½ teaspoon salt
- 1 tablespoon chopped fresh cilantro
- freshly ground black pepper

Directions:

1. Place the black beans in a large bowl and smash them slightly with the back of a fork. Add the ground turkey, red onion, Jalapeño pepper, breadcrumbs, chili powder and cayenne pepper. Season with salt. Mix with your hands to combine all the ingredients and then shape them into 2 patties. Brush both sides of the burger patties with a little olive or vegetable oil.
2. Preheat the air fryer to 380°F.
3. Transfer the burgers to the air fryer basket and air-fry for 20 minutes, flipping them over halfway through the cooking process. Top the burgers with the pepper jack cheese (securing the slices to the burgers with a toothpick) for the last 2 minutes of the cooking process.
4. While the burgers are cooking, make the cumin avocado spread. Place the avocado, lime juice, cumin and salt in food processor and process until smooth. (For a chunkier spread, you can mash this by hand in a bowl.) Stir in the cilantro and season with freshly ground black pepper. Chill the spread until you are ready to serve.
5. When the burgers have finished cooking, remove them from the air fryer and let them rest on a plate, covered gently with aluminum foil. Brush a little olive oil on the insides of the burger rolls. Place the rolls, cut side up, into the air fryer basket and air-fry at 400°F for 1 minute to toast and warm them.
6. Spread the cumin-avocado spread on the rolls and build your burgers with lettuce and sliced tomatoes and any other ingredient you like. Serve warm with a side of sweet potato fries.

Saucy Chicken Thighs

Servings: 4

Cooking Time: 35 Minutes

Ingredients:

- 8 boneless, skinless chicken thighs
- 1 tbsp Italian seasoning
- Salt and pepper to taste
- 2 garlic cloves, minced
- ½ tsp apple cider vinegar
- ½ cup honey
- ¼ cup Dijon mustard

Directions:

1. Preheat air fryer to 400°F. Season the chicken with Italian seasoning, salt, and black pepper. Place in the greased frying basket and Bake for 15 minutes, flipping once halfway through cooking.
2. While the chicken is cooking, add garlic, honey, vinegar, and Dijon mustard in a saucepan and stir-fry over medium heat for 4 minutes or until the sauce has thickened and warmed through. Transfer the thighs to a serving dish and drizzle with honey-mustard sauce. Serve and enjoy!

Beef , pork & Lamb Recipes

Pepper Steak

Servings: 4
Cooking Time: 30 Minutes
Ingredients:

- 2 tablespoons cornstarch
- 1 tablespoon sugar
- ¾ cup beef broth
- ¼ cup hoisin sauce
- 3 tablespoons soy sauce
- 1 teaspoon sesame oil
- ½ teaspoon freshly ground black pepper
- 1½ pounds boneless New York strip steaks, sliced into ½-inch strips
- 1 onion, sliced
- 3 small bell peppers, red, yellow and green, sliced

Directions:

1. Whisk the cornstarch and sugar together in a large bowl to break up any lumps in the cornstarch. Add the beef broth and whisk until combined and smooth. Stir in the hoisin sauce, soy sauce, sesame oil and freshly ground black pepper. Add the beef, onion and peppers, and toss to coat. Marinate the beef and vegetables at room temperature for 30 minutes, stirring a few times to keep meat and vegetables coated.
2. Preheat the air fryer to 350°F.
3. Transfer the beef, onion, and peppers to the air fryer basket with tongs, reserving the marinade. Air-fry the beef and vegetables for 30 minutes, stirring well two or three times during the cooking process.
4. While the beef is air-frying, bring the reserved marinade to a simmer in a small saucepan over medium heat on the stovetop. Simmer for 5 minutes until the sauce thickens.
5. When the steak and vegetables have finished cooking, transfer them to a serving platter. Pour the hot sauce over the pepper steak and serve with white rice.

Extra Crispy Country-style Pork Riblets

Servings: 3
Cooking Time: 30 Minutes
Ingredients:

- ⅓ cup Tapioca flour
- 2½ tablespoons Chile powder
- ¾ teaspoon Table salt (optional)
- 1¼ pounds Boneless country-style pork ribs, cut into 1½-inch chunks
- Vegetable oil spray

Directions:

1. Preheat the air fryer to 375°F .
2. Mix the tapioca flour, chile powder, and salt (if using) in a large bowl until well combined. Add the country-style rib chunks and toss well to coat thoroughly.
3. When the machine is at temperature, gently shake off any excess tapioca coating from the chunks. Generously coat them on all sides with vegetable oil spray. Arrange the chunks in the basket in one (admittedly fairly tight) layer. The pieces may touch. Air-fry for 30 minutes, rearranging the pieces at the 10- and 20-minute marks to expose any touching bits, until very crisp and well browned.
4. Gently pour the contents of the basket onto a wire rack. Cool for 5 minutes before serving.

Chicken-fried Steak

Servings: 2
Cooking Time: 12 Minutes
Ingredients:

- 1½ cups All-purpose flour
- 2 Large egg(s)
- 2 tablespoons Regular or low-fat sour cream
- 2 tablespoons Worcestershire sauce
- 2 ¼-pound thin beef cube steak(s)
- Vegetable oil spray

Directions:

1. Preheat the air fryer to 400°F.
2. Set up and fill two shallow soup plates or small pie plates on your counter: one for the flour; and one for the egg(s), whisked with the sour cream and Worcestershire sauce until uniform.
3. Dredge a piece of beef in the flour, coating it well on both sides and even along the edge. Shake off any excess; then dip the meat in the egg mixture, coating both sides

while retaining the flour on the meat. Let any excess egg mixture slip back into the rest. Dredge the meat in the flour once again, coating all surfaces well. Gently shake off the excess coating and set the steak aside if you're coating another steak or two. Once done, coat the steak(s) on both sides with the vegetable oil spray.

4. Set the steak(s) in the basket. If there's more than one steak, make sure they do not overlap or even touch, although the smallest gap between them is enough to get them crunchy. Air-fry undisturbed for 6 minutes.

5. Use kitchen tongs to pick up one of the steaks. Coat it again on both sides with vegetable oil spray. Turn it upside down and set it back in the basket with that same regard for the space between them in larger batches. Repeat with any other steaks. Continue air-frying undisturbed for 6 minutes, or until golden brown and crunchy.

6. Use kitchen tongs to transfer the steak(s) to a wire rack. Cool for 5 minutes before serving.

Friday Night Cheeseburgers

Servings: 4

Cooking Time: 20 Minutes

Ingredients:

- 1 lb ground beef
- 1 tsp Worcestershire sauce
- 1 tbsp allspice
- Salt and pepper to taste
- 4 cheddar cheese slices
- 4 buns

Directions:

1. Preheat air fryer to 360°F. Combine beef, Worcestershire sauce, allspice, salt and pepper in a large bowl. Divide into 4 equal portions and shape into patties. Place the burgers in the greased frying basket and Air Fry for 8 minutes. Flip and cook for another 3-4 minutes. Top each burger with cheddar cheese and cook for another minute so the cheese melts. Transfer to a bun and serve.

Red Curry Flank Steak

Servings: 4

Cooking Time: 18 Minutes

Ingredients:

- 3 tablespoons red curry paste
- ¼ cup olive oil
- 2 teaspoons grated fresh ginger
- 2 tablespoons soy sauce
- 2 tablespoons rice wine vinegar
- 3 scallions, minced
- 1½ pounds flank steak
- fresh cilantro (or parsley) leaves

Directions:

1. Mix the red curry paste, olive oil, ginger, soy sauce, rice vinegar and scallions together in a bowl. Place the flank steak in a shallow glass dish and pour half the marinade over the steak. Pierce the steak several times with a fork or meat tenderizer to let the marinade penetrate the meat. Turn the steak over, pour the remaining marinade over the top and pierce the steak several times again. Cover and marinate the steak in the refrigerator for 6 to 8 hours.

2. When you are ready to cook, remove the steak from the refrigerator and let it sit at room temperature for 30 minutes.

3. Preheat the air fryer to 400°F.

4. Cut the flank steak in half so that it fits more easily into the air fryer and transfer both pieces to the air fryer basket. Pour the marinade over the steak. Air-fry for 18 minutes, depending on your preferred degree of doneness of the steak (12 minutes = medium rare). Flip the steak over halfway through the cooking time.

5. When your desired degree of doneness has been reached, remove the steak to a cutting board and let it rest for 5 minutes before slicing. Thinly slice the flank steak against the grain of the meat. Transfer the slices to a serving platter, pour any juice from the bottom of the air fryer over the sliced flank steak and sprinkle the fresh cilantro on top.

Sriracha Short Ribs

Servings: 4

Cooking Time: 15 Minutes

Ingredients:

- 2 tsp sesame seeds
- 8 pork short ribs
- ½ cup soy sauce
- ¼ cup rice wine vinegar
- ½ cup chopped onion
- 2 garlic cloves, minced
- 1 tbsp sesame oil

- 1 tsp sriracha
- 4 scallions, thinly sliced
- Salt and pepper to taste

Directions:

1. Put short ribs in a resealable bag along with soy sauce, vinegar, onion, garlic, sesame oil, Sriracha, half of the scallions, salt, and pepper. Seal the bag and toss to coat. Refrigerate for one hour.
2. Preheat air fryer to 380°F. Place the short ribs in the air fryer. Bake for 8-10 minutes, flipping once until crisp. When the ribs are done, garnish with remaining scallions and sesame seeds. Serve and enjoy!

Paprika Fried Beef

Servings: 4

Cooking Time: 30 Minutes

Ingredients:

- Celery salt to taste
- 4 beef cube steaks
- ½ cup milk
- 1 cup flour
- 2 tsp paprika
- 1 egg
- 1 cup bread crumbs
- 2 tbsp olive oil

Directions:

1. Preheat air fryer to 350°F. Place the cube steaks in a zipper sealed bag or between two sheets of cling wrap. Gently pound the steaks until they are slightly thinner. Set aside. In a bowl, mix together milk, flour, paprika, celery salt, and egg until just combined. In a separate bowl, mix together the crumbs and olive oil. Take the steaks and dip them into the buttermilk batter, shake off some of the excess, and return to a plate for 5 minutes. Next, dip the steaks in the bread crumbs, patting the crumbs into both sides. Air Fry the steaks until the crust is crispy and brown, 12-16 minutes. Serve warm.

Tarragon Pork Tenderloin

Servings: 4

Cooking Time: 25 Minutes

Ingredients:

- ½ tsp dried tarragon
- 1 lb pork tenderloin, sliced
- Salt and pepper to taste
- 2 tbsp Dijon mustard
- 1 clove garlic, minced
- 1 cup bread crumbs
- 2 tbsp olive oil

Directions:

1. Preheat air fryer to 390°F. Using a rolling pin, pound the pork slices until they are about ¾ inch thick. Season both sides with salt and pepper. Coat the pork with mustard and season with garlic and tarragon. In a shallow bowl, mix bread crumbs and olive oil. Dredge the pork with the bread crumbs, pressing firmly, so that it adheres. Put the pork in the frying basket and Air Fry until the pork outside is brown and crisp, 12-14 minutes. Serve warm.

Lamb Chops

Servings: 2

Cooking Time: 20 Minutes

Ingredients:

- 2 teaspoons oil
- ½ teaspoon ground rosemary
- ½ teaspoon lemon juice
- 1 pound lamb chops, approximately 1-inch thick
- salt and pepper
- cooking spray

Directions:

1. Mix the oil, rosemary, and lemon juice together and rub into all sides of the lamb chops. Season to taste with salt and pepper.
2. For best flavor, cover lamb chops and allow them to rest in the fridge for 20 minutes.
3. Spray air fryer basket with nonstick spray and place lamb chops in it.
4. Cook at 360°F for approximately 20minutes. This will cook chops to medium. The meat will be juicy but have no remaining pink. Cook for a minute or two longer for well done chops. For rare chops, stop cooking after about 12minutes and check for doneness.

Pork Cutlets With Almond-lemon Crust

Servings: 3
Cooking Time: 14 Minutes
Ingredients:

- ¾ cup Almond flour
- ¾ cup Plain dried bread crumbs (gluten-free, if a concern)
- 1½ teaspoons Finely grated lemon zest
- 1¼ teaspoons Table salt
- ¾ teaspoon Garlic powder
- ¾ teaspoon Dried oregano
- 1 Large egg white(s)
- 2 tablespoons Water
- 3 6-ounce center-cut boneless pork loin chops (about ¾ inch thick)
- Olive oil spray

Directions:

1. Preheat the air fryer to 375°F .
2. Mix the almond flour, bread crumbs, lemon zest, salt, garlic powder, and dried oregano in a large bowl until well combined.
3. Whisk the egg white(s) and water in a shallow soup plate or small pie plate until uniform.
4. Dip a chop in the egg white mixture, turning it to coat all sides, even the ends. Let any excess egg white mixture slip back into the rest, then set it in the almond flour mixture. Turn it several times, pressing gently to coat it evenly. Generously coat the chop with olive oil spray, then set aside to dip and coat the remaining chop(s).
5. Set the chops in the basket with as much air space between them as possible. Air-fry undisturbed for 12 minutes, or until browned and crunchy. You may need to add 2 minutes to the cooking time if the machine is at 360°F.
6. Use kitchen tongs to transfer the chops to a wire rack. Cool for a few minutes before serving.

Leftover Roast Beef Risotto

Servings: 4
Cooking Time: 30 Minutes
Ingredients:

- ½ chopped red bell pepper
- ½ chopped cooked roast beef
- 3 tbsp grated Parmesan
- 2 tsp butter, melted
- 1 shallot, finely chopped
- 3 garlic cloves, minced
- ¾ cup short-grain rice
- 1¼ cups beef broth

Directions:

1. Preheat air fryer to 390°F. Add the melted butter, shallot, garlic, and red bell pepper to a baking pan and stir to combine. Air Fry for 2 minutes, or until the vegetables are crisp-tender. Remove from the air fryer and stir in the rice, broth, and roast beef. Put the cooking pan back into the fryer and Bake for 18-22 minutes, stirring once during cooking until the rice is al dente and the beef is cooked through. Sprinkle with Parmesan and serve.

Argentinian Steak Asado Salad

Servings: 2
Cooking Time: 35 Minutes
Ingredients:

- 1 jalapeño pepper, sliced thin
- ¼ cup shredded pepper Jack cheese
- 1 avocado, peeled and pitted
- ¼ cup diced tomatoes
- ½ diced shallot
- 2 tsp chopped cilantro
- 2 tsp lime juice
- ½ lb flank steak
- 1 garlic clove, minced
- 1 tsp ground cumin
- Salt and pepper to taste
- ¼ lime
- 3 cups mesclun mix
- ½ cup pico de gallo

Directions:

1. Mash the avocado in a small bowl. Add tomatoes, shallot, cilantro, lime juice, salt, and pepper. Set aside. Season the steak with garlic, salt, pepper, and cumin.
2. Preheat air fryer to 400°F. Put the steak into the greased frying basket. Bake 8-10 minutes, flipping once until your desired doneness. Remove and let rest. Squeeze the lime over the steak and cut into thin slices. For one serving, plate

half of mesclun, 2 tbsp of cheese, and ¼ cup guacamole. Place half of the steak slices on top t, then add ¼ cup pico de gallo and jalapeño if desired.

6. Meanwhile, place the buns inside the air fryer and toast them for 3 minutes.
7. To assemble the burgers, place the hamburger on one side of the bun, top with onion compote and ¼ cup arugula, and then place the other half of the bun on top.

Steakhouse Burgers With Red Onion Compote

Servings: 4
Cooking Time: 22 Minutes
Ingredients:

- 1½ pounds lean ground beef
- 2 cloves garlic, minced and divided
- 1 teaspoon Worcestershire sauce
- 1 teaspoon sea salt, divided
- ½ teaspoon black pepper
- 1 tablespoon extra-virgin olive oil
- 1 red onion, thinly sliced
- ¼ cup balsamic vinegar
- 1 teaspoon sugar
- 1 tablespoon tomato paste
- 2 tablespoons mayonnaise
- 2 tablespoons sour cream
- 4 brioche hamburger buns
- 1 cup arugula

Directions:

1. In a large bowl, mix together the ground beef, 1 of the minced garlic cloves, the Worcestershire sauce, ½ teaspoon of the salt, and the black pepper. Form the meat into 1-inch-thick patties. Make a dent in the center (this helps the center cook evenly). Let the meat sit for 15 minutes.
2. Meanwhile, in a small saucepan over medium heat, cook the olive oil and red onion for 4 minutes, stirring frequently to avoid burning. Add in the balsamic vinegar, sugar, and tomato paste, and cook for an additional 3 minutes, stirring frequently. Transfer the onion compote to a small bowl.
3. Preheat the air fryer to 350°F.
4. In another small bowl, mix together the remaining minced garlic, the mayonnaise, and the sour cream. Spread the mayo mixture on the insides of the brioche buns.
5. Cook the hamburgers for 6 minutes, flip the burgers, and cook an additional 2 to 6 minutes. Check the internal temperature to avoid under- or overcooking. Hamburgers should be cooked to at least 160°F. After cooking, cover with foil and let the meat rest for 5 minutes.

Lamb Meatballs With Quick Tomato Sauce

Servings: 4
Cooking Time: 8 Minutes
Ingredients:

- ½ small onion, finely diced
- 1 clove garlic, minced
- 1 pound ground lamb
- 2 tablespoons fresh parsley, finely chopped (plus more for garnish)
- 2 teaspoons fresh oregano, finely chopped
- 2 tablespoons milk
- 1 egg yolk
- salt and freshly ground black pepper
- ½ cup crumbled feta cheese, for garnish
- Tomato Sauce:
- 2 tablespoons butter
- 1 clove garlic, smashed
- pinch crushed red pepper flakes
- ¼ teaspoon ground cinnamon
- 1 (28-ounce) can crushed tomatoes
- salt, to taste

Directions:

1. Combine all ingredients for the meatballs in a large bowl and mix just until everything is combined. Shape the mixture into 1½-inch balls or shape the meat between two spoons to make quenelles (little three-sided footballs).
2. Preheat the air fryer to 400°F.
3. While the air fryer is Preheating, start the quick tomato sauce. Place the butter, garlic and red pepper flakes in a sauté pan and heat over medium heat on the stovetop. Let the garlic sizzle a little, but before the butter starts to brown, add the cinnamon and tomatoes. Bring to a simmer and simmer for 15 minutes. Season to taste with salt (but not too much as the feta that you will be sprinkling on at the end will be salty).

4. Brush the bottom of the air fryer basket with a little oil and transfer the meatballs to the air fryer basket in one layer, air-frying in batches if necessary.
5. Air-fry at 400°F for 8 minutes, giving the basket a shake once during the cooking process to turn the meatballs over.
6. To serve, spoon a pool of the tomato sauce onto plates and add the meatballs in a decorative manner. Sprinkle the feta cheese on top and garnish with more fresh parsley. Serve immediately.

Pepperoni Pockets

Servings: 4
Cooking Time: 8 Minutes
Ingredients:

- 4 bread slices, 1-inch thick
- olive oil for misting
- 24 slices pepperoni (about 2 ounces)
- 1 ounce roasted red peppers, drained and patted dry
- 1 ounce Pepper Jack cheese cut into 4 slices
- pizza sauce (optional)

Directions:

1. Spray both sides of bread slices with olive oil.
2. Stand slices upright and cut a deep slit in the top to create a pocket—almost to the bottom crust but not all the way through.
3. Stuff each bread pocket with 6 slices of pepperoni, a large strip of roasted red pepper, and a slice of cheese.
4. Place bread pockets in air fryer basket, standing up. Cook at 360°F for 8 minutes, until filling is heated through and bread is lightly browned. Serve while hot as is or with pizza sauce for dipping.

Rib Eye Bites With Mushrooms

Servings: 4
Cooking Time: 30 Minutes
Ingredients:

- 1 ¼ lb boneless rib-eye or sirloin steak, cubed
- 8 oz button mushrooms, halved
- 4 tbsp rapeseed oil
- 1 onion, chopped
- 2 garlic cloves, minced
- Salt and pepper to taste
- 2 tsp lime juice
- 1 tsp dried marjoram
- 2 tbsp chopped parsley

Directions:

1. Preheat the air fryer to 400°F. Combine the rapeseed oil, onion, mushrooms, garlic, steak cubes, salt, pepper, lime juice, marjoram, and parsley in a baking pan. Put it in the frying basket and Bake for 12-15 minutes, stirring once or twice to ensure an even cooking, and until golden brown. The veggies should be tender. Serve hot.

Vietnamese Beef Lettuce Wraps

Servings: 4
Cooking Time: 12 Minutes
Ingredients:

- ⅓ cup low-sodium soy sauce*
- 2 teaspoons fish sauce*
- 2 teaspoons brown sugar
- 1 tablespoon chili paste
- juice of 1 lime
- 2 cloves garlic, minced
- 2 teaspoons fresh ginger, minced
- 1 pound beef sirloin
- Sauce
- ⅓ cup low-sodium soy sauce*
- juice of 2 limes
- 1 tablespoon mirin wine
- 2 teaspoons chili paste
- Serving
- 1 head butter lettuce
- ½ cup julienned carrots
- ½ cup julienned cucumber
- ½ cup sliced radishes, sliced into half moons
- 2 cups cooked rice noodles
- ⅓ cup chopped peanuts

Directions:

1. Combine the soy sauce, fish sauce, brown sugar, chili paste, lime juice, garlic and ginger in a bowl. Slice the beef into thin slices, then cut those slices in half. Add the beef to the marinade and marinate for 1 to 3 hours in the refrigerator.

When you are ready to cook, remove the steak from the refrigerator and let it sit at room temperature for 30 minutes.

2. Preheat the air fryer to 400°F.
3. Transfer the beef and marinade to the air fryer basket. Air-fry at 400°F for 12 minutes, shaking the basket a few times during the cooking process.
4. While the beef is cooking, prepare a wrap-building station. Combine the soy sauce, lime juice, mirin wine and chili paste in a bowl and transfer to a little pouring vessel. Separate the lettuce leaves from the head of lettuce and put them in a serving bowl. Place the carrots, cucumber, radish, rice noodles and chopped peanuts all in separate serving bowls.
5. When the beef has finished cooking, transfer it to another serving bowl and invite your guests to build their wraps. To build the wraps, place some beef in a lettuce leaf and top with carrots, cucumbers, some rice noodles and chopped peanuts. Drizzle a little sauce over top, fold the lettuce around the ingredients and enjoy!

Stuffed Cabbage Rolls

Servings: 4

Cooking Time: 50 Minutes

Ingredients:

- ½ cup long-grain brown rice
- 12 green cabbage leaves
- 1 lb ground beef
- 4 garlic cloves, minced
- Salt and pepper to taste
- 1 tsp ground cinnamon
- ½ tsp ground cumin
- 2 tbsp chopped mint
- 1 lemon, juiced and zested
- ½ cup beef broth
- 1 tbsp olive oil
- 2 tbsp parsley, chopped

Directions:

1. Place a large pot of salted water over medium heat and bring to a boil. Add the cabbage leaves and boil them for 3 minutes. Remove from the water and set aside. Combine the ground beef, rice, garlic, salt, pepper, cinnamon, cumin, mint, lemon juice and zest in a bowl.
2. Preheat air fryer to 360°F. Divide the beef mixture between the cabbage leaves and roll them up. Place the finished rolls into a greased baking dish. Pour the beef broth over the cabbage rolls and then brush the tops with olive oil. Put the casserole dish into the frying basket and Bake for 30 minutes. Top with parsley and enjoy!

Perfect Strip Steaks

Servings: 2

Cooking Time: 17 Minutes

Ingredients:

- 1½ tablespoons Olive oil
- 1½ tablespoons Minced garlic
- 2 teaspoons Ground black pepper
- 1 teaspoon Table salt
- 2 ¾-pound boneless beef strip steak(s)

Directions:

1. Preheat the air fryer to 375°F (or 380°F or 390°F, if one of these is the closest setting).
2. Mix the oil, garlic, pepper, and salt in a small bowl, then smear this mixture over both sides of the steak(s).
3. When the machine is at temperature, put the steak(s) in the basket with as much air space as possible between them for the larger batch. They should not overlap or even touch. That said, even just a ¼-inch between them will work. Air-fry for 12 minutes, turning once, until an instant-read meat thermometer inserted into the thickest part of a steak registers 127°F for rare (not USDA-approved). Or air-fry for 15 minutes, turning once, until an instant-read meat thermometer registers 145°F for medium (USDA-approved). If the machine is at 390°F, the steaks may cook 2 minutes more quickly than the stated timing.
4. Use kitchen tongs to transfer the steak(s) to a wire rack. Cool for 5 minutes before serving.

Garlic And Oregano Lamb Chops

Servings: 4

Cooking Time: 17 Minutes

Ingredients:

- 1½ tablespoons Olive oil
- 1 tablespoon Minced garlic
- 1 teaspoon Dried oregano
- 1 teaspoon Finely minced orange zest
- ¾ teaspoon Fennel seeds

- ¾ teaspoon Table salt
- ¾ teaspoon Ground black pepper
- 6 4-ounce, 1-inch-thick lamb loin chops

Directions:

1. Mix the olive oil, garlic, oregano, orange zest, fennel seeds, salt, and pepper in a large bowl. Add the chops and toss well to coat. Set aside as the air fryer heats, tossing one more time.
2. Preheat the air fryer to 400°F.
3. Set the chops bone side down in the basket (that is, so they stand up on their bony edge) with as much air space between them as possible. Air-fry undisturbed for 14 minutes for medium-rare, or until an instant-read meat thermometer inserted into the thickest part of a chop (without touching bone) registers 132°F (not USDA-approved). Or air-fry undisturbed for 17 minutes for well done, or until an instant-read meat thermometer registers 145°F (USDA-approved).
4. Use kitchen tongs to transfer the chops to a wire rack. Cool for 5 minutes before serving.

Italian Sausage Bake

Servings: 4

Cooking Time: 25 Minutes

Ingredients:

- 1 cup red bell pepper, strips
- ¾ lb Italian sausage, sliced
- ½ cup minced onions
- 3 tbsp brown sugar
- 1/3 cup ketchup
- 2 tbsp mustard
- 2 tbsp apple cider vinegar
- ½ cup chicken broth

Directions:

1. Preheat air fryer to 350°F. Combine the Italian sausage, bell pepper, and minced onion into a bowl. Stir well. Mix together brown sugar, ketchup, mustard, apple cider vinegar, and chicken broth in a small bowl. Pour over the sausage. Place the bowl in the air fryer, and Bake until the sausage is hot, the vegetables are tender, and the sauce is bubbling and thickened, 10-15 minutes. Serve and enjoy!

Lazy Mexican Meat Pizza

Servings: 4

Cooking Time: 35 Minutes

Ingredients:

- 1 ¼ cups canned refried beans
- 2 cups shredded cheddar
- ½ cup chopped cilantro
- 2/3 cup salsa
- 1 red bell pepper, chopped
- 1 sliced jalapeño
- 1 pizza crust
- 16 meatballs, halved

Directions:

1. Preheat the air fryer to 375°F. Combine the refried beans, salsa, jalapeño, and bell pepper in a bowl and spread on the pizza crust. Top with meatball halves and sprinkle with cheddar cheese. Put the pizza in the greased frying basket and Bake for 7-10 minutes until hot and the cheese is brown. Sprinkle with the fresh cilantro and serve.

Smokehouse-style Beef Ribs

Servings: 3

Cooking Time: 25 Minutes

Ingredients:

- ¼ teaspoon Mild smoked paprika
- ¼ teaspoon Garlic powder
- ¼ teaspoon Onion powder
- ¼ teaspoon Table salt
- ¼ teaspoon Ground black pepper
- 3 10- to 12-ounce beef back ribs (not beef short ribs)

Directions:

1. Preheat the air fryer to 350°F .
2. Mix the smoked paprika, garlic powder, onion powder, salt, and pepper in a small bowl until uniform. Massage and pat this mixture onto the ribs.
3. When the machine is at temperature, set the ribs in the basket in one layer, turning them on their sides if necessary, sort of like they're spooning but with at least ¼ inch air space between them. Air-fry for 25 minutes, turning once, until deep brown and sizzling.
4. Use kitchen tongs to transfer the ribs to a wire rack. Cool for 5 minutes before serving.

Mushroom & Quinoa-stuffed Pork Loins

Servings: 3
Cooking Time: 25 Minutes
Ingredients:

- 3 boneless center-cut pork loins, pocket cut in each loin
- ½ cup diced white mushrooms
- 1 tsp vegetable oil
- 3 bacon slices, diced
- ½ onion, peeled and diced
- 1 cup baby spinach
- Salt and pepper to taste
- ½ cup cooked quinoa
- ½ cup mozzarella cheese

Directions:
1. Warm the oil in a skillet over medium heat. Add the bacon and cook for 3 minutes until the fat is rendered but not crispy. Add in onion and mushrooms and stir-fry for 3 minutes until the onions are translucent. Stir in spinach, salt, and pepper and cook for 1 minute until the spinach wilts. Set aside and toss in quinoa.
2. Preheat air fryer at 350ºF. Stuff quinoa mixture into each pork loin and sprinkle with mozzarella cheese. Place them in the frying basket and Air Fry for 11 minutes. Let rest onto a cutting board for 5 minutes before serving.

California Burritos

Servings: 4
Cooking Time: 17 Minutes
Ingredients:

- 1 pound sirloin steak, sliced thin
- 1 teaspoon dried oregano
- 1 teaspoon ground cumin
- ½ teaspoon garlic powder
- 16 tater tots
- ⅓ cup sour cream
- ½ lime, juiced
- 2 tablespoons hot sauce
- 1 large avocado, pitted
- 1 teaspoon salt, divided
- 4 large (8- to 10-inch) flour tortillas
- ½ cup shredded cheddar cheese or Monterey jack
- 2 tablespoons avocado oil

Directions:
1. Preheat the air fryer to 380°F.
2. Season the steak with oregano, cumin, and garlic powder. Place the steak on one side of the air fryer and the tater tots on the other side. (It's okay for them to touch, because the flavors will all come together in the burrito.) Cook for 8 minutes, toss, and cook an additional 4 to 6 minutes.
3. Meanwhile, in a small bowl, stir together the sour cream, lime juice, and hot sauce.
4. In another small bowl, mash together the avocado and season with ½ teaspoon of the salt, to taste.
5. To assemble the burrito, lay out the tortillas, equally divide the meat amongst the tortillas. Season the steak equally with the remaining ½ teaspoon salt. Then layer the mashed avocado and sour cream mixture on top. Top each tortilla with 4 tater tots and finish each with 2 tablespoons cheese. Roll up the sides and, while holding in the sides, roll up the burrito. Place the burritos in the air fryer basket and brush with avocado oil (working in batches as needed); cook for 3 minutes or until lightly golden on the outside.

Peachy Pork Chops

Servings:2
Cooking Time: 20 Minutes
Ingredients:

- 2 tbsp peach preserves
- 2 tbsp tomato paste
- 1 tbsp Dijon mustard
- 1 tsp BBQ sauce
- 1 tbsp lime juice
- 1 tbsp olive oil
- 2 cloves garlic, minced
- 2 pork chops

Directions:
1. Whisk all ingredients in a bowl until well mixed and let chill covered in the fridge for 30 minutes. Preheat air fryer to 350ºF. Place pork chops in the frying basket and Air Fry for 12 minutes or until cooked through and tender. Transfer the chops to a cutting board and let sit for 5 minutes before serving.

Rack Of Lamb With Pistachio Crust

Servings: 2

Cooking Time: 19 Minutes

Ingredients:

- ½ cup finely chopped pistachios
- 3 tablespoons panko breadcrumbs
- 1 teaspoon chopped fresh rosemary
- 2 teaspoons chopped fresh oregano
- salt and freshly ground black pepper
- 1 tablespoon olive oil
- 1 rack of lamb, bones trimmed of fat and frenched
- 1 tablespoon Dijon mustard

Directions:

1. Preheat the air fryer to 380°F.
2. Combine the pistachios, breadcrumbs, rosemary, oregano, salt and pepper in a small bowl. Drizzle in the olive oil and stir to combine.
3. Season the rack of lamb with salt and pepper on all sides and transfer it to the air fryer basket with the fat side facing up. Air-fry the lamb for 12 minutes. Remove the lamb from the air fryer and brush the fat side of the lamb rack with the Dijon mustard. Coat the rack with the pistachio mixture, pressing the breadcrumbs onto the lamb with your hands and rolling the bottom of the rack in any of the crumbs that fall off.
4. Return the rack of lamb to the air fryer and air-fry for another 3 to 7 minutes or until an instant read thermometer reads 140°F for medium. Add or subtract a couple of minutes for lamb that is more or less well cooked. (Your time will vary depending on how big the rack of lamb is.)
5. Let the lamb rest for at least 5 minutes. Then, slice into chops and serve.

Suwon Pork Meatballs

Servings: 4

Cooking Time: 30 Minutes

Ingredients:

- 1 lb ground pork
- 1 egg
- 1 tsp cumin
- 1 tbsp gochujang
- 1 tsp tamari
- ¼ tsp ground ginger
- ¼ cup bread crumbs
- 1 scallion, sliced
- 4 tbsp plum jam
- 1 tsp toasted sesame seeds

Directions:

1. Preheat air fryer at 350ºF. In a bowl, combine all ingredients, except scallion greens, sesame seeds and plum jam. Form mixture into meatballs. Place meatballs in the greased frying basket and Air Fry for 8 minutes, flipping once. Garnish with scallion greens, plum jam and toasted sesame seeds to serve.

Sage Pork With Potatoes

Servings: 4

Cooking Time: 30 Minutes

Ingredients:

- 2 cups potatoes
- 2 tsp olive oil
- 1 lb pork tenderloin, cubed
- 1 onion, chopped
- 1 red bell pepper, chopped
- 2 garlic cloves, minced
- ½ tsp dried sage
- ½ tsp fennel seeds, crushed
- 2 tbsp chicken broth

Directions:

1. Preheat air fryer to 370°F. Add the potatoes and olive oil to a bowl and toss to coat. Transfer them to the frying basket and Air Fry for 15 minutes. Remove the bowl. Add the pork, onion, red bell pepper, garlic, sage, and fennel seeds, to the potatoes, add chicken broth and stir gently. Return the bowl to the frying basket and cook for 10 minutes. Be sure to shake the basket at least once. The pork should be cooked through and the potatoes soft and crispy. Serve immediately.

Fish And Seafood Recipes

Black Olive & Shrimp Salad

Servings: 4
Cooking Time: 15 Minutes
Ingredients:

- 1 lb cleaned shrimp, deveined
- ½ cup olive oil
- 4 garlic cloves, minced
- 1 tbsp balsamic vinegar
- ¼ tsp cayenne pepper
- ¼ tsp dried basil
- ¼ tsp salt
- ¼ tsp onion powder
- 1 tomato, diced
- ¼ cup black olives

Directions:

1. Preheat air fryer to 380°F. Place the olive oil, garlic, balsamic, cayenne, basil, onion powder and salt in a bowl and stir to combine. Divide the tomatoes and black olives between 4 small ramekins. Top with shrimp and pour a quarter of the oil mixture over the shrimp. Bake for 6-8 minutes until the shrimp are cooked through. Serve.

Southern Shrimp With Cocktail Sauce

Servings: 2
Cooking Time: 20 Minutes
Ingredients:

- ½ lb raw shrimp, tail on, deveined and shelled
- 1 cup ketchup
- 2 tbsp prepared horseradish
- 1 tbsp lemon juice
- ½ tsp Worcestershire sauce
- 1/8 tsp chili powder
- Salt and pepper to taste
- 1/3 cup flour
- 2 tbsp cornstarch
- ¼ cup milk
- 1 egg
- ½ cup bread crumbs
- 1 tbsp Cajun seasoning
- 1 lemon, cut into pieces

Directions:

1. In a small bowl, whisk the ketchup, horseradish, lemon juice, Worcestershire sauce, chili powder, salt, and pepper. Let chill covered in the fridge until ready to use. Preheat air fryer at 375ºF. In a bowl, mix the flour, cornstarch, and salt. In another bowl, beat the milk and egg and in a third bowl, combine breadcrumbs and Cajun seasoning.
2. Roll the shrimp in the flour mixture, shake off excess flour. Then, dip in the egg, shake off excess egg. Finally, dredge in the breadcrumbs mixture. Place shrimp in the greased frying basket and Air Fry for 8 minutes, flipping once. Serve with cocktail sauce and lemon slices.

Crab Cakes On A Budget

Servings: 4
Cooking Time: 12 Minutes
Ingredients:

- 8 ounces imitation crabmeat
- 4 ounces leftover cooked fish (such as cod, pollock, or haddock)
- 2 tablespoons minced green onion
- 2 tablespoons minced celery
- ¾ cup crushed saltine cracker crumbs
- 2 tablespoons light mayonnaise
- 1 teaspoon prepared yellow mustard
- 1 tablespoon Worcestershire sauce, plus 2 teaspoons
- 2 teaspoons dried parsley flakes
- ½ teaspoon dried dill weed, crushed
- ½ teaspoon garlic powder
- ½ teaspoon Old Bay Seasoning
- ½ cup panko breadcrumbs
- oil for misting or cooking spray

Directions:

1. Use knives or a food processor to finely shred crabmeat and fish.
2. In a large bowl, combine all ingredients except panko and oil. Stir well.
3. Shape into 8 small, fat patties.

4. Carefully roll patties in panko crumbs to coat. Spray both sides with oil or cooking spray.
5. Place patties in air fryer basket and cook at 390°F for 12 minutes or until golden brown and crispy.

Mediterranean Salmon Cakes

Servings:4
Cooking Time: 30 Minutes
Ingredients:

- ¼ cup heavy cream
- 5 tbsp mayonnaise
- 2 cloves garlic, minced
- ¼ tsp caper juice
- 2 tsp lemon juice
- 1 tbsp capers
- 1 can salmon
- 2 tsp lemon zest
- 1 egg
- ¼ minced red bell peppers
- ½ cup flour
- ⅛ tsp salt
- 2 tbsp sliced green olives

Directions:

1. Combine heavy cream, 2 tbsp of mayonnaise, garlic, caper juices, capers, and lemon juice in a bowl. Place the resulting caper sauce in the fridge until ready to use.
2. Preheat air fryer to 400ºF. Combine canned salmon, lemon zest, egg, remaining mayo, bell peppers, flour, and salt in a bowl. Form into 8 patties. Place the patties in the greased frying basket and Air Fry for 10 minutes, turning once. Let rest for 5 minutes before drizzling with lemon sauce. Garnish with green olives to serve.

Black Cod With Grapes, Fennel, Pecans And Kale

Servings: 2
Cooking Time: 15 Minutes
Ingredients:

- 2 (6- to 8-ounce) fillets of black cod (or sablefish)
- salt and freshly ground black pepper
- olive oil
- 1 cup grapes, halved
- 1 small bulb fennel, sliced ¼-inch thick
- ½ cup pecans
- 3 cups shredded kale
- 2 teaspoons white balsamic vinegar or white wine vinegar
- 2 tablespoons extra virgin olive oil

Directions:

1. Preheat the air fryer to 400°F.
2. Season the cod fillets with salt and pepper and drizzle, brush or spray a little olive oil on top. Place the fish, presentation side up (skin side down), into the air fryer basket. Air-fry for 10 minutes.
3. When the fish has finished cooking, remove the fillets to a side plate and loosely tent with foil to rest.
4. Toss the grapes, fennel and pecans in a bowl with a drizzle of olive oil and season with salt and pepper. Add the grapes, fennel and pecans to the air fryer basket and air-fry for 5 minutes at 400°F, shaking the basket once during the cooking time.
5. Transfer the grapes, fennel and pecans to a bowl with the kale. Dress the kale with the balsamic vinegar and olive oil, season to taste with salt and pepper and serve along side the cooked fish.

Crab Stuffed Salmon Roast

Servings: 4
Cooking Time: 20 Minutes
Ingredients:

- 1 (1½-pound) salmon fillet
- salt and freshly ground black pepper
- 6 ounces crabmeat
- 1 teaspoon finely chopped lemon zest
- 1 teaspoon Dijon mustard
- 1 tablespoon chopped fresh parsley, plus more for garnish
- 1 scallion, chopped
- ¼ teaspoon salt
- olive oil

Directions:

1. Prepare the salmon fillet by butterflying it. Slice into the thickest side of the salmon, parallel to the countertop and

along the length of the fillet. Don't slice all the way through to the other side – stop about an inch from the edge. Open the salmon up like a book. Season the salmon with salt and freshly ground black pepper.

2. Make the crab filling by combining the crabmeat, lemon zest, mustard, parsley, scallion, salt and freshly ground black pepper in a bowl. Spread this filling in the center of the salmon. Fold one side of the salmon over the filling. Then fold the other side over on top.

3. Transfer the rolled salmon to the center of a piece of parchment paper that is roughly 6- to 7-inches wide and about 12-inches long. The parchment paper will act as a sling, making it easier to put the salmon into the air fryer. Preheat the air fryer to 370°F. Use the parchment paper to transfer the salmon roast to the air fryer basket and tuck the ends of the paper down beside the salmon. Drizzle a little olive oil on top and season with salt and pepper.

4. Air-fry the salmon at 370°F for 20 minutes.

5. Remove the roast from the air fryer and let it rest for a few minutes. Then, slice it, sprinkle some more lemon zest and parsley (or fresh chives) on top and serve.

Curried Sweet-and-spicy Scallops

Servings:3

Cooking Time: 5 Minutes

Ingredients:

- 6 tablespoons Thai sweet chili sauce
- 2 cups (from about 5 cups cereal) Crushed Rice Krispies or other rice-puff cereal
- 2 teaspoons Yellow curry powder, purchased or homemade (see here)
- 1 pound Sea scallops
- Vegetable oil spray

Directions:

1. Preheat the air fryer to 400°F.
2. Set up and fill two shallow soup plates or small pie plates on your counter: one for the chili sauce and one for crumbs, mixed with the curry powder.
3. Dip a scallop into the chili sauce, coating it on all sides. Set it in the cereal mixture and turn several times to coat evenly. Gently shake off any excess and set the scallop on a cutting board. Continue dipping and coating the remaining scallops. Coat them all on all sides with the vegetable oil spray.
4. Set the scallops in the basket with as much air space between them as possible. Air-fry undisturbed for 5 minutes, or until lightly browned and crunchy.
5. Remove the basket. Set aside for 2 minutes to let the coating set up. Then gently pour the contents of the basket onto a platter and serve at once.

Restaurant-style Breaded Shrimp

Servings: 2

Cooking Time: 35 Minutes

Ingredients:

- ½ lb fresh shrimp, peeled
- 2 eggs, beaten
- ½ cup breadcrumbs
- ½ onion, finely chopped
- ½ tsp ground ginger
- ½ tsp garlic powder
- ½ tsp turmeric
- ½ tsp red chili powder
- Salt and pepper to taste
- ½ tsp amchur powder

Directions:

1. Preheat air fryer to 350°F. Place the beaten eggs in a bowl and dip in the shrimp. Blend the bread crumbs with all the dry ingredients in another bowl. Add in the shrimp and toss to coat. Place the coated shrimp in the greased frying basket. Air Fry for 12-14 minutes until the breaded crust of the shrimp is golden brown. Toss the basket two or three times during the cooking time. Serve.

Salmon Croquettes

Servings: 4

Cooking Time: 8 Minutes

Ingredients:

- 1 tablespoon oil
- ½ cup breadcrumbs
- 1 14.75-ounce can salmon, drained and all skin and fat removed
- 1 egg, beaten
- ⅓ cup coarsely crushed saltine crackers (about 8 crackers)

- ½ teaspoon Old Bay Seasoning
- ½ teaspoon onion powder
- ½ teaspoon Worcestershire sauce

Directions:

1. Preheat air fryer to 390°F.
2. In a shallow dish, mix oil and breadcrumbs until crumbly.
3. In a large bowl, combine the salmon, egg, cracker crumbs, Old Bay, onion powder, and Worcestershire. Mix well and shape into 8 small patties about ½-inch thick.
4. Gently dip each patty into breadcrumb mixture and turn to coat well on all sides.
5. Cook at 390°F for 8minutes or until outside is crispy and browned.

Fish Sticks For Grown-ups

Servings: 4
Cooking Time: 6 Minutes
Ingredients:

- 1 pound fish fillets
- ½ teaspoon hot sauce
- 1 tablespoon coarse brown mustard
- 1 teaspoon Worcestershire sauce
- salt
- Crumb Coating
- ¾ cup panko breadcrumbs
- ¼ cup stone-ground cornmeal
- ¼ teaspoon salt
- oil for misting or cooking spray

Directions:

1. Cut fish fillets crosswise into slices 1-inch wide.
2. Mix the hot sauce, mustard, and Worcestershire sauce together to make a paste and rub on all sides of the fish. Season to taste with salt.
3. Mix crumb coating ingredients together and spread on a sheet of wax paper.
4. Roll the fish fillets in the crumb mixture.
5. Spray all sides with olive oil or cooking spray and place in air fryer basket in a single layer.
6. Cook at 390°F for 6 minutes, until fish flakes easily.

Tilapia Al Pesto

Servings:4
Cooking Time: 25 Minutes
Ingredients:

- 4 tilapia fillets
- 1 egg
- 2 tbsp buttermilk
- 1 cup crushed cornflakes
- Salt and pepper to taste
- 4 tsp pesto
- 2 tbsp butter, melted
- 4 lemon wedges

Directions:

1. Preheat air fryer to 350ºF. Whisk egg and buttermilk in a bowl. In another bowl, combine cornflakes, salt, and pepper. Spread 1 tsp of pesto on each tilapia fillet, then tightly roll the fillet from one short end to the other. Secure with a toothpick. Dip each fillet in the egg mixture and dredge in the cornflake mixture. Place fillets in the greased frying basket, drizzle with melted butter, and Air Fry for 6 minutes. Let rest onto a serving dish for 5 minutes before removing the toothpicks. Serve with lemon wedges.

Tuscan Salmon

Servings: 4
Cooking Time: 15 Minutes
Ingredients:

- 2 tbsp olive oil
- 4 salmon fillets
- ½ tsp salt
- ¼ tsp red pepper flakes
- 1 tsp chopped dill
- 2 tomatoes, diced
- ¼ cup sliced black olives
- 4 lemon slices

Directions:

1. Preheat air fryer to 380°F. Lightly brush the olive oil on both sides of the salmon fillets and season them with salt, red flakes, and dill. Put the fillets in a single layer in the frying basket, then layer the tomatoes and black olives over the top. Top each fillet with a lemon slice. Bake for 8 minutes. Serve and enjoy!

Lemony Tuna Steaks

Servings: 4
Cooking Time: 20 Minutes
Ingredients:

- ½ tbsp olive oil
- 1 garlic clove, minced
- Salt to taste
- ¼ tsp jalapeno powder
- 1 tbsp lemon juice
- 1 tbsp chopped cilantro
- ½ tbsp chopped dill
- 4 tuna steaks
- 1 lemon, thinly sliced

Directions:

1. Stir olive oil, garlic, salt, jalapeno powder, lemon juice, and cilantro in a wide bowl. Coat the tuna on all sides in the mixture. Cover and marinate for at least 20 minutes
2. Preheat air fryer to 380°F. Arrange the tuna on a single layer in the greased frying basket and throw out the excess marinade. Bake for 6-8 minutes. Remove the basket and let the tuna rest in it for 5 minutes. Transfer to plates and garnish with lemon slices. Serve sprinkled with dill.

Classic Shrimp Po'boy Sandwiches

Servings: 4
Cooking Time: 20 Minutes
Ingredients:

- 1 lb peeled shrimp, deveined
- 1 egg
- ½ cup flour
- ¾ cup cornmeal
- Salt and pepper to taste
- ½ cup mayonnaise
- 1 tsp Creole mustard
- 1 tsp Worcestershire sauce
- 1 tsp minced garlic
- 2 tbsp sweet pickle relish
- 1 tsp Louisiana hot sauce
- ½ tsp Creole seasoning
- 4 rolls
- 2 cups shredded lettuce
- 8 tomato slices

Directions:

1. Preheat air fryer to 400°F. Set up three small bowls. In the first, add flour. In the second, beat the egg. In the third, mix cornmeal with salt and pepper. First dip the shrimp in the flour, then dredge in the egg, then dip in the cornmeal. Place in the greased frying basket. Air Fry for 8 minutes, flipping once until crisp. Let cool slightly.
2. While the shrimp is cooking, mix mayonnaise, mustard, Worcestershire, garlic, pickle relish juice, hot sauce, and Creole seasoning in a small bowl. Set aside. To assemble the po'boys, split rolls along the crease and spread the inside with remoulade. Layer ¼ of the shrimp, ½ cup shredded lettuce, and 2 slices of tomato. Serve and enjoy!

Cheesy Tuna Tower

Servings:2
Cooking Time: 15 Minutes
Ingredients:

- ½ cup grated mozzarella
- 1 can tuna in water
- ¼ cup mayonnaise
- 2 tsp yellow mustard
- 1 tbsp minced dill pickle
- 1 tbsp minced celery
- 1 tbsp minced green onion
- Salt and pepper to taste
- 4 tomato slices
- 8 avocado slices

Directions:

1. Preheat air fryer to 350ºF. In a bowl, combine tuna, mayonnaise, mustard, pickle, celery, green onion, salt, and pepper. Cut a piece of parchment paper to fit the bottom of the frying basket. Place tomato slices on paper in a single layer and top with 2 avocado slices. Share tuna salad over avocado slices and top with mozzarella cheese. Place the towers in the frying basket and Bake for 4 minutes until the cheese starts to brown. Serve warm.

Corn & Shrimp Boil

Servings: 4
Cooking Time: 40 Minutes
Ingredients:

- 8 frozen "mini" corn on the cob
- 1 tbsp smoked paprika
- 2 tsp dried thyme
- 1 tsp dried marjoram
- 1 tsp sea salt
- 1 tsp garlic powder
- 1 tsp onion powder
- 1 tsp cayenne pepper
- 1 lb baby potatoes, halved
- 1 tbsp olive oil
- 1 lb peeled shrimp, deveined
- 1 avocado, sliced

Directions:

1. Preheat the air fryer to 370°F.Combine the paprika, thyme, marjoram, salt, garlic, onion, and cayenne and mix well. Pour into a small glass jar. Add the potatoes, corn, and olive oil to the frying basket and sprinkle with 2 tsp of the spice mix and toss. Air Fry for 15 minutes, shaking the basket once until tender. Remove and set aside. Put the shrimp in the frying basket and sprinkle with 2 tsp of the spice mix. Air Fry for 5-8 minutes, shaking once until shrimp are tender and pink. Combine all the ingredients in the frying basket and sprinkle with 2 tsp of the spice mix. Toss to coat and cook for 1-2 more minutes or until hot. Serve topped with avocado.

Horseradish Crusted Salmon

Servings: 2
Cooking Time: 14 Minutes
Ingredients:

- 2 (5-ounce) salmon fillets
- salt and freshly ground black pepper
- 2 teaspoons Dijon mustard
- ½ cup panko breadcrumbs*
- 2 tablespoons prepared horseradish
- ½ teaspoon finely chopped lemon zest
- 1 tablespoon olive oil
- 1 tablespoon chopped fresh parsley

Directions:

1. Preheat the air fryer to 360°F.
2. Season the salmon with salt and freshly ground black pepper. Then spread the Dijon mustard on the salmon, coating the entire surface.
3. Combine the breadcrumbs, horseradish, lemon zest and olive oil in a small bowl. Spread the mixture over the top of the salmon and press down lightly with your hands, adhering it to the salmon using the mustard as "glue".
4. Transfer the salmon to the air fryer basket and air-fry at 360°F for 14 minutes (depending on how thick your fillet is) or until the fish feels firm to the touch. Sprinkle with the parsley.

Salmon

Servings: 4
Cooking Time: 8 Minutes
Ingredients:

- Marinade
- 3 tablespoons low-sodium soy sauce
- 3 tablespoons rice vinegar
- 3 tablespoons ketchup
- 3 tablespoons olive oil
- 3 tablespoons brown sugar
- 1 teaspoon garlic powder
- ½ teaspoon ground ginger
- 4 salmon fillets (½-inch thick, 3 to 4 ounces each)
- cooking spray

Directions:

1. Mix all marinade ingredients until well blended.
2. Place salmon in sealable plastic bag or shallow container with lid. Pour marinade over fish and turn to coat well. Refrigerate for 30minutes.
3. Drain marinade, and spray air fryer basket with cooking spray.
4. Place salmon in basket, skin-side down.
5. Cook at 360°F for 10 minutes, watching closely to avoid overcooking. Salmon is done when just beginning to flake and still very moist.

Chinese Fish Noodle Bowls

Servings: 4

Cooking Time: 40 Minutes

Ingredients:

- 1 can crushed pineapple, drained
- 1 shallot, minced
- 2 tbsp chopped cilantro
- 2 ½ tsp lime juice
- 1 tbsp honey
- Salt and pepper to taste
- 1 ½ cups grated red cabbage
- ¼ chopped green beans
- 2 grated baby carrots
- ½ tsp granulated sugar
- 2 tbsp mayonnaise
- 1 clove garlic, minced
- 8 oz cooked rice noodles
- 2 tsp sesame oil
- 1 tsp sesame seeds
- 4 cod fillets
- 1 tsp Chinese five-spice

Directions:

1. Preheat air fryer at 350ºF. Combine the pineapple, shallot, 1 tbsp of cilantro, honey, 2 tsp of lime juice, salt, and black pepper in a bowl. Let chill the salsa covered in the fridge until ready to use. Mix the cabbage, green beans, carrots, sugar, remaining lime juice, mayonnaise, garlic, salt, and pepper in a bowl. Let chill covered in the fridge until ready to use. In a bowl, toss cooked noodles and sesame oil, stirring occasionally to avoid sticking.
2. Sprinkle cod fillets with salt and five-spice. Place them in the greased frying basket and Air Fry for 10 minutes until the fish is opaque and flakes easily with a fork. Divide noodles into 4 bowls, top each with salsa, slaw, and fish. Serve right away sprinkled with another tbsp of cilantro and sesame seeds.

Bacon-wrapped Scallops

Servings: 4

Cooking Time: 8 Minutes

Ingredients:

- 16 large scallops
- 8 bacon strips
- ½ teaspoon black pepper
- ¼ teaspoon smoked paprika

Directions:

1. Pat the scallops dry with a paper towel. Slice each of the bacon strips in half. Wrap 1 bacon strip around 1 scallop and secure with a toothpick. Repeat with the remaining scallops. Season the scallops with pepper and paprika.
2. Preheat the air fryer to 350°F.
3. Place the bacon-wrapped scallops in the air fryer basket and cook for 4 minutes, shake the basket, cook another 3 minutes, shake the basket, and cook another 1 to 3 to minutes. When the bacon is crispy, the scallops should be cooked through and slightly firm, but not rubbery. Serve immediately.

Five Spice Red Snapper With Green Onions And Orange Salsa

Servings: 2

Cooking Time: 8 Minutes

Ingredients:

- 2 oranges, peeled, segmented and chopped
- 1 tablespoon minced shallot
- 1 to 3 teaspoons minced red Jalapeño or Serrano pepper
- 1 tablespoon chopped fresh cilantro
- lime juice, to taste
- salt, to taste
- 2 (5- to 6-ounce) red snapper fillets
- ½ teaspoon Chinese five spice powder
- salt and freshly ground black pepper
- vegetable or olive oil, in a spray bottle
- 4 green onions, cut into 2-inch lengths

Directions:

1. Start by making the salsa. Cut the peel off the oranges, slicing around the oranges to expose the flesh. Segment the oranges by cutting in between the membranes of the orange. Chop the segments roughly and combine in a bowl with the shallot, Jalapeño or Serrano pepper, cilantro, lime juice and salt. Set the salsa aside.
2. Preheat the air fryer to 400°F.
3. Season the fish fillets with the five-spice powder, salt and freshly ground black pepper. Spray both sides of the fish fillets with oil. Toss the green onions with a little oil.

4. Transfer the fish to the air fryer basket and scatter the green onions around the fish. Air-fry at 400°F for 8 minutes.
5. Remove the fish from the air fryer, along with the fried green onions. Serve with white rice and a spoonful of the salsa on top.

Super Crunchy Flounder Fillets

Servings:2
Cooking Time: 6 Minutes
Ingredients:

- ½ cup All-purpose flour or tapioca flour
- 1 Large egg white(s)
- 1 tablespoon Water
- ¾ teaspoon Table salt
- 1 cup Plain panko bread crumbs (gluten-free, if a concern)
- 2 4-ounce skinless flounder fillet(s)
- Vegetable oil spray

Directions:

1. Preheat the air fryer to 400°F.
2. Set up and fill three shallow soup plates or small pie plates on your counter: one for the flour; one for the egg white(s), beaten with the water and salt until foamy; and one for the bread crumbs.
3. Dip one fillet in the flour, turning it to coat both sides. Gently shake off any excess flour, then dip the fillet in the egg white mixture, turning it to coat. Let any excess egg white mixture slip back into the rest, then set the fish in the bread crumbs. Turn it several times, gently pressing it into the crumbs to create an even crust. Generously coat both sides of the fillet with vegetable oil spray. If necessary, set it aside and continue coating the remaining fillet(s) in the same way.
4. Set the fillet(s) in the basket. If working with more than one fillet, they should not touch, although they may be quite close together, depending on the basket's size. Air-fry undisturbed for 6 minutes, or until lightly browned and crunchy.
5. Use a nonstick-safe spatula to transfer the fillet(s) to a wire rack. Cool for only a minute or two before serving.

Stuffed Shrimp

Servings: 4
Cooking Time: 12 Minutes Per Batch
Ingredients:

- 16 tail-on shrimp, peeled and deveined (last tail section intact)
- ¾ cup crushed panko breadcrumbs
- oil for misting or cooking spray
- Stuffing
- 2 6-ounce cans lump crabmeat
- 2 tablespoons chopped shallots
- 2 tablespoons chopped green onions
- 2 tablespoons chopped celery
- 2 tablespoons chopped green bell pepper
- ½ cup crushed saltine crackers
- 1 teaspoon Old Bay Seasoning
- 1 teaspoon garlic powder
- ¼ teaspoon ground thyme
- 2 teaspoons dried parsley flakes
- 2 teaspoons fresh lemon juice
- 2 teaspoons Worcestershire sauce
- 1 egg, beaten

Directions:

1. Rinse shrimp. Remove tail section (shell) from 4 shrimp, discard, and chop the meat finely.
2. To prepare the remaining 12 shrimp, cut a deep slit down the back side so that the meat lies open flat. Do not cut all the way through.
3. Preheat air fryer to 360°F.
4. Place chopped shrimp in a large bowl with all of the stuffing ingredients and stir to combine.
5. Divide stuffing into 12 portions, about 2 tablespoons each.
6. Place one stuffing portion onto the back of each shrimp and form into a ball or oblong shape. Press firmly so that stuffing sticks together and adheres to shrimp.
7. Gently roll each stuffed shrimp in panko crumbs and mist with oil or cooking spray.
8. Place 6 shrimp in air fryer basket and cook at 360°F for 10minutes. Mist with oil or spray and cook 2 minutes longer or until stuffing cooks through inside and is crispy outside.
9. Repeat step 8 to cook remaining shrimp.

Lemon-dill Salmon Burgers

Servings: 4
Cooking Time: 8 Minutes
Ingredients:

- 2 (6-ounce) fillets of salmon, finely chopped by hand or in a food processor
- 1 cup fine breadcrumbs
- 1 teaspoon freshly grated lemon zest
- 2 tablespoons chopped fresh dill weed
- 1 teaspoon salt
- freshly ground black pepper
- 2 eggs, lightly beaten
- 4 brioche or hamburger buns
- lettuce, tomato, red onion, avocado, mayonnaise or mustard, to serve

Directions:

1. Preheat the air fryer to 400°F.
2. Combine all the ingredients in a bowl. Mix together well and divide into four balls. Flatten the balls into patties, making an indentation in the center of each patty with your thumb (this will help the burger stay flat as it cooks) and flattening the sides of the burgers so that they fit nicely into the air fryer basket.
3. Transfer the burgers to the air fryer basket and air-fry for 4 minutes. Flip the burgers over and air-fry for another 3 to 4 minutes, until nicely browned and firm to the touch.
4. Serve on soft brioche buns with your choice of topping – lettuce, tomato, red onion, avocado, mayonnaise or mustard.

Spiced Salmon Croquettes

Servings: 6
Cooking Time: 20 Minutes
Ingredients:

- 1 can Alaskan pink salmon, bones removed
- 1 lime, zested
- 1 red chili, minced
- 2 tbsp cilantro, chopped
- 1 egg, beaten
- ½ cup bread crumbs
- 2 scallions, diced
- 1 tsp garlic powder
- Salt and pepper to taste

Directions:

1. Preheat air fryer to 400°F. Mix salmon, beaten egg, bread crumbs and scallions in a large bowl. Add garlic, lime, red chili, cilantro, salt and pepper. Divide into 6 even portions and shape into patties. Place them in the greased frying basket and Air Fry for 7 minutes. Flip them and cook for 4 minutes or until golden. Serve.

Mexican-style Salmon Stir-fry

Servings: 4
Cooking Time: 30 Minutes
Ingredients:

- 12 oz salmon fillets, cubed
- 1 red bell pepper, chopped
- 1 red onion, chopped
- 1 jalapeño pepper, minced
- ¼ cup salsa
- 2 tbsp tomato juice
- 2 tsp peanut oil
- 1 tsp chili powder
- 2 tbsp cilantro, chopped

Directions:

1. Preheat air fryer to 360°F. Mix salmon, bell pepper, onion, jalapeño, salsa, tomato juice, peanut oil, and chili powder in a bowl and put it into the air fryer. Air Fry for 12-14 minutes until the salmon is firm and the veggies are crispy and soft, stirring once. Serve topped with cilantro.

Easy Asian-style Tuna

Servings: 4
Cooking Time: 25 Minutes
Ingredients:

- 1 jalapeño pepper, minced
- ½ tsp Chinese five-spice
- 4 tuna steaks
- ½ tsp toasted sesame oil
- 2 garlic cloves, grated
- 1 tbsp grated fresh ginger
- Black pepper to taste

- 2 tbsp lemon juice

Directions:

1. Preheat air fryer to 380°F. Pour sesame oil over the tuna steaks and let them sit while you make the marinade. Combine the jalapeño, garlic, ginger, five-spice powder, black pepper, and lemon juice in a bowl, then brush the mix on the fish. Let it sit for 10 minutes. Air Fry the tuna in the fryer for 6-11 minutes until it is cooked through and flakes easily when pressed with a fork. Serve warm.

Lemon-dill Salmon With Green Beans

Servings: 4

Cooking Time: 20 Minutes

Ingredients:

- 20 halved cherry tomatoes
- 4 tbsp butter
- 4 garlic cloves, minced
- ¼ cup chopped dill
- Salt and pepper to taste
- 4 wild-caught salmon fillets
- ¼ cup white wine
- 1 lemon, thinly sliced
- 1 lb green beans, trimmed
- 2 tbsp chopped parsley

Directions:

1. Preheat air fryer to 390°F. Combine butter, garlic, dill, wine, salt, and pepper in a small bowl. Spread the seasoned butter over the top of the salmon. Arrange the fish in a single layer in the frying basket. Top with ½ of the lemon slices and surround the fish with green beans and tomatoes. Bake for 12-15 minutes until salmon is cooked and vegetables are tender. Top with parsley and serve with lemon slices on the side.

Mahi-mahi "burrito" Fillets

Servings:3

Cooking Time: 10 Minutes

Ingredients:

- 1 Large egg white
- 1½ cups (6 ounces) Crushed corn tortilla chips (gluten-free, if a concern)
- 1 tablespoon Chile powder
- 3 5-ounce skinless mahi-mahi fillets
- 6 tablespoons Canned refried beans
- Vegetable oil spray

Directions:

1. Preheat the air fryer to 400°F.
2. Set up and fill two shallow soup plates or small pie plates on your counter: one with the egg white, beaten until foamy; and one with the crushed tortilla chips.
3. Gently rub ½ teaspoon chile powder on each side of each fillet.
4. Spread (or maybe smear) 1 tablespoon refried beans over both sides and the edges of a fillet. Dip the fillet in the egg white, turning to coat it on both sides. Let any excess egg white slip back into the rest, then set the fillet in the crushed tortilla chips. Turn several times, pressing gently to coat it evenly. Coat the fillet on all sides with the vegetable oil spray, then set it aside. Prepare the remaining fillet(s) in the same way.
5. When the machine is at temperature, set the fillets in the basket with as much air space between them as possible. Air-fry undisturbed for 10 minutes, or until crisp and browned.
6. Use a nonstick-safe spatula to transfer the fillets to a serving platter or plates. Cool for only a minute or so, then serve hot.

Vegetarians Recipes

Golden Breaded Mushrooms

Servings: 2
Cooking Time: 20 Minutes
Ingredients:

- 2 cups crispy rice cereal
- 1 tsp nutritional yeast
- 2 tsp garlic powder
- 1tsp dried oregano
- 1 tsp dried basil
- Salt to taste
- 1 tbsp Dijon mustard
- 1 tbsp mayonnaise
- ¼ cup milk
- 8 oz whole mushrooms
- 4 tbsp chili sauce
- 3 tbsp mayonnaise

Directions:

1. Preheat air fryer at 350ºF. Blend rice cereal, garlic powder, oregano, basil, nutritional yeast, and salt in a food processor until it gets a breadcrumb consistency. Set aside in a bowl. Mix the mustard, mayonnaise, and milk in a bowl. Dip mushrooms in the mustard mixture; shake off any excess. Then, dredge them in the breadcrumbs; shake off any excess. Places mushrooms in the greased frying basket and Air Fry for 7 minutes, shaking once. Mix the mayonnaise with chili sauce in a small bowl. Serve the mushrooms with the dipping sauce on the side.

Vegetarian Eggplant "pizzas"

Servings:4
Cooking Time: 25 Minutes
Ingredients:

- ½ cup diced baby bella mushrooms
- 3 tbsp olive oil
- ¼ cup diced onions
- ½ cup pizza sauce
- 1 eggplant, sliced
- 1 tsp salt
- 1 cup shredded mozzarella
- ¼ cup chopped oregano

Directions:

1. Warm 2 tsp of olive oil in a skillet over medium heat. Add in onion and mushrooms and stir-fry for 4 minutes until tender. Stir in pizza sauce. Turn the heat off.
2. Preheat air fryer to 375ºF. Brush the eggplant slices with the remaining olive oil on both sides. Lay out slices on a large plate and season with salt. Then, top with the sauce mixture and shredded mozzarella. Place the eggplant pizzas in the frying basket and Air Fry for 5 minutes. Garnish with oregano to serve.

Fennel Tofu Bites

Servings: 4
Cooking Time: 35 Minutes
Ingredients:

- 1/3 cup vegetable broth
- 2 tbsp tomato sauce
- 2 tsp soy sauce
- 1 tbsp nutritional yeast
- 1 tsp Italian seasoning
- 1 tsp granulated sugar
- 1 tsp ginger grated
- ½ tsp fennel seeds
- ½ tsp garlic powder
- Salt and pepper to taste
- 14 oz firm tofu, cubed
- 2/3 cup bread crumbs
- 1 tsp Italian seasoning
- 2 tsp toasted sesame seeds
- 1 cup marinara sauce, warm

Directions:

1. In a large bowl, whisk the vegetable broth, soy sauce, ginger, tomato sauce, nutritional yeast, Italian seasoning, sugar, fennel seeds, garlic powder, salt and black pepper. Toss in tofu to coat. Let marinate covered in the fridge for 30 minutes, tossing once.
2. Preheat air fryer at 350ºF. Mix the breadcrumbs, Italian seasoning, and salt in a bowl. Strain marinade from tofu cubes and dredge them in the breadcrumb mixture. Place tofu cubes in the greased frying basket and Air Fry for 10 minutes, turning once. Serve sprinkled with sesame seeds and marinara sauce on the side.

Pizza Portobello Mushrooms

Servings: 2

Cooking Time: 18 Minutes

Ingredients:

- 2 portobello mushroom caps, gills removed (see Figure 13-1)
- 1 teaspoon extra-virgin olive oil
- ¼ cup diced onion
- 1 teaspoon minced garlic
- 1 medium zucchini, shredded
- 1 teaspoon dried oregano
- ½ teaspoon black pepper
- ¼ teaspoon salt
- ⅓ cup marinara sauce
- ¼ cup shredded part-skim mozzarella cheese
- ¼ teaspoon red pepper flakes
- 2 tablespoons Parmesan cheese
- 2 tablespoons chopped basil

Directions:

1. Preheat the air fryer to 370°F.
2. Lightly spray the mushrooms with an olive oil mist and place into the air fryer to cook for 10 minutes, cap side up.
3. Add the olive oil to a pan and sauté the onion and garlic together for about 2 to 4 minutes. Stir in the zucchini, oregano, pepper, and salt, and continue to cook. When the zucchini has cooked down (usually about 4 to 6 minutes), add in the marinara sauce. Remove from the heat and stir in the mozzarella cheese.
4. Remove the mushrooms from the air fryer basket when cooking completes. Reset the temperature to 350°F.
5. Using a spoon, carefully stuff the mushrooms with the zucchini marinara mixture.
6. Return the stuffed mushrooms to the air fryer basket and cook for 5 to 8 minutes, or until the cheese is lightly browned. You should be able to easily insert a fork into the mushrooms when they're cooked.
7. Remove the mushrooms and sprinkle the red pepper flakes, Parmesan cheese, and fresh basil over the top.
8. Serve warm.

Meatless Kimchi Bowls

Servings:4

Cooking Time: 20 Minutes

Ingredients:

- 2 cups canned chickpeas
- 1 carrot, julienned
- 6 scallions, sliced
- 1 zucchini, diced
- 2 tbsp coconut aminos
- 2 tsp sesame oil
- 1 tsp rice vinegar
- 2 tsp granulated sugar
- 1 tbsp gochujang
- ¼ tsp salt
- ½ cup kimchi
- 2 tsp roasted sesame seeds

Directions:

1. Preheat air fryer to 350ºF. Combine all ingredients, except for the kimchi, 2 scallions, and sesame seeds, in a baking pan. Place the pan in the frying basket and Air Fry for 6 minutes. Toss in kimchi and cook for 2 more minutes. Divide between 2 bowls and garnish with the remaining scallions and sesame seeds. Serve immediately.

Harissa Veggie Fries

Servings: 4

Cooking Time: 55 Minutes

Ingredients:

- 1 pound red potatoes, cut into rounds
- 1 onion, diced
- 1 green bell pepper, diced
- 1 red bell pepper, diced
- 2 tbsp olive oil
- Salt and pepper to taste
- ¾ tsp garlic powder
- ¾ tsp harissa seasoning

Directions:

1. Combine all ingredients in a large bowl and mix until potatoes are well coated and seasoned. Preheat air fryer to 350°F. Pour all of the contents in the bowl into the frying basket. Bake for 35 minutes, shaking every 10 minutes, until golden brown and soft. Serve hot.

Farfalle With White Sauce

Servings: 4
Cooking Time: 30 Minutes

Ingredients:

- 4 cups cauliflower florets
- 1 medium onion, chopped
- 8 oz farfalle pasta
- 2 tbsp chives, minced
- ½ cup cashew pieces
- 1 tbsp nutritional yeast
- 2 large garlic cloves, peeled
- 2 tbsp fresh lemon juice
- Salt and pepper to taste

Directions:

1. Preheat air fryer to 390°F. Put the cauliflower in the fryer, spray with oil, and Bake for 8 minutes. Remove the basket, stir, and add the onion. Roast for 10 minutes or until the cauliflower is golden and the onions soft. Cook the farfalle pasta according to the package directions. Set aside. Put the roasted cauliflower and onions along with the cashews, 1 ½ of cups water, yeast, garlic, lemon, salt, and pepper in a blender. Blend until creamy. Pour a large portion of the sauce on top of the warm pasta and add the minced scallions. Serve.

Arancini With Marinara

Servings: 6
Cooking Time: 15 Minutes

Ingredients:

- 2 cups cooked rice
- 1 cup grated Parmesan cheese
- 1 egg, whisked
- ¼ teaspoon dried thyme
- ½ teaspoon dried oregano
- ½ teaspoon dried basil
- ½ teaspoon dried parsley
- 1 teaspoon salt
- ¼ teaspoon paprika
- 1 cup breadcrumbs
- 4 ounces mozzarella, cut into 24 cubes
- 2 cups marinara sauce

Directions:

1. In a large bowl, mix together the rice, Parmesan cheese, and egg.
2. In another bowl, mix together the thyme, oregano, basil, parsley, salt, paprika, and breadcrumbs.
3. Form 24 rice balls with the rice mixture. Use your thumb to make an indentation in the center and stuff 1 cube of mozzarella in the center of the rice; close the ball around the cheese.
4. Roll the rice balls in the seasoned breadcrumbs until all are coated.
5. Preheat the air fryer to 400°F.
6. Place the rice balls in the air fryer basket and coat with cooking spray. Cook for 8 minutes, shake the basket, and cook another 7 minutes.
7. Heat the marinara sauce in a saucepan until warm. Serve sauce as a dip for arancini.

Roasted Vegetable Lasagna

Servings: 6
Cooking Time: 55 Minutes

Ingredients:

- 1 zucchini, sliced
- 1 yellow squash, sliced
- 8 ounces mushrooms, sliced
- 1 red bell pepper, cut into 2-inch strips
- 1 tablespoon olive oil
- 2 cups ricotta cheese
- 2 cups grated mozzarella cheese, divided
- 1 egg
- 1 teaspoon salt
- freshly ground black pepper
- ¼ cup shredded carrots
- ½ cup chopped fresh spinach
- 8 lasagna noodles, cooked
- Béchamel Sauce:
- 3 tablespoons butter
- 3 tablespoons flour
- 2½ cups milk
- ½ cup grated Parmesan cheese
- ½ teaspoon salt
- freshly ground black pepper
- pinch of ground nutmeg

Directions:

1. Preheat the air fryer to 400°F.

2. Toss the zucchini, yellow squash, mushrooms and red pepper in a large bowl with the olive oil and season with salt and pepper. Air-fry for 10 minutes, shaking the basket once or twice while the vegetables cook.

3. While the vegetables are cooking, make the béchamel sauce and cheese filling. Melt the butter in a medium saucepan over medium-high heat on the stovetop. Add the flour and whisk, cooking for a couple of minutes. Add the milk and whisk vigorously until smooth. Bring the mixture to a boil and simmer until the sauce thickens. Stir in the Parmesan cheese and season with the salt, pepper and nutmeg. Set the sauce aside.

4. Combine the ricotta cheese, 1¼ cups of the mozzarella cheese, egg, salt and pepper in a large bowl and stir until combined. Fold in the carrots and spinach.

5. When the vegetables have finished cooking, build the lasagna. Use a baking dish that is 6 inches in diameter and 4 inches high. Cover the bottom of the baking dish with a little béchamel sauce. Top with two lasagna noodles, cut to fit the dish and overlapping each other a little. Spoon a third of the ricotta cheese mixture and then a third of the roasted veggies on top of the noodles. Pour ½ cup of béchamel sauce on top and then repeat these layers two more times: noodles – cheese mixture – vegetables – béchamel sauce. Sprinkle the remaining mozzarella cheese over the top. Cover the dish with aluminum foil, tenting it loosely so the aluminum doesn't touch the cheese.

6. Lower the dish into the air fryer basket using an aluminum foil sling (fold a piece of aluminum foil into a strip about 2-inches wide by 24-inches long). Fold the ends of the aluminum foil over the top of the dish before returning the basket to the air fryer. Air-fry for 45 minutes, removing the foil for the last 2 minutes, to slightly brown the cheese on top.

7. Let the lasagna rest for at least 20 minutes to set up a little before slicing into it and serving.

Berbere Eggplant Dip

Servings:4

Cooking Time: 35 Minutes

Ingredients:

- 1 eggplant, halved lengthwise
- 3 tsp olive oil
- 2 tsp pine nuts
- ¼ cup tahini
- 1 tbsp lemon juice
- 2 cloves garlic, minced
- ¼ tsp berbere seasoning
- ⅛ tsp ground cumin
- Salt and pepper to taste
- 1 tbsp chopped parsley

Directions:

1. Preheat air fryer to 370ºF. Brush the eggplant with some olive oil. With a fork, pierce the eggplant flesh a few times. Place them, flat sides-down, in the frying basket. Air Fry for 25 minutes. Transfer the eggplant to a cutting board and let cool for 3 minutes until easy to handle. Place pine nuts in the frying basket and Air Fry for 2 minutes, shaking every 30 seconds. Set aside in a bowl.

2. Scoop out the eggplant flesh and add to a food processor. Add in tahini, lemon juice, garlic, berbere seasoning, cumin, salt, and black pepper and pulse until smooth. Transfer to a serving bowl. Scatter with toasted pine nuts, parsley, and the remaining olive oil. Serve immediately.

Quinoa & Black Bean Stuffed Peppers

Servings: 4

Cooking Time: 30 Minutes

Ingredients:

- ½ cup vegetable broth
- ½ cup quinoa
- 1 can black beans
- ½ cup diced red onion
- 1 garlic clove, minced
- ½ tsp salt
- ½ tsp ground cumin
- ¼ tsp paprika
- ¼ tsp ancho chili powder
- 4 bell peppers, any color
- ½ cup grated cheddar
- ¼ cup chopped cilantro
- ½ cup red enchilada sauce

Directions:

1. Add vegetable broth and quinoa to a small saucepan over medium heat. Bring to a boil, then cover and let it simmer for 5 minutes. Turn off the heat.

2. Preheat air fryer to 350°F. Transfer quinoa to a medium bowl and stir in black beans, onion, red enchilada sauce,

ancho chili powder, garlic, salt, cumin, and paprika. Cut the top ¼-inch off the bell peppers. Remove seeds and membranes. Scoop quinoa filling into each pepper and top with cheddar cheese. Transfer peppers to the frying basket and bake for 10 minutes until peppers are soft and filling is heated through. Garnish with cilantro. Serve warm along with salsa. Enjoy!

Mushroom Lasagna

Servings: 4

Cooking Time: 40 Minutes

Ingredients:

- 2 tbsp olive oil
- 1 zucchini, diced
- ½ cup diced mushrooms
- ¼ cup diced onion
- 1 cup marinara sauce
- 1 cup ricotta cheese
- 1/3 cup grated Parmesan
- 1 egg
- 2 tsp Italian seasoning
- 2 tbsp fresh basil, chopped
- ½ tsp thyme
- 1 tbsp red pepper flakes
- ½ tsp salt
- 5 lasagna noodle sheets
- 1 cup grated mozzarella

Directions:

1. Heat the oil in a skillet over medium heat. Add zucchini, mushrooms, 1 tbsp of basil, thyme, red pepper flakes and onion and cook for 4 minutes until the veggies are tender. Toss in marinara sauce, and bring it to a bowl. Then, low the heat and simmer for 3 minutes.
2. Preheat air fryer at 375ºF. Combine ricotta cheese, Parmesan cheese, egg, Italian seasoning, and salt in a bowl. Spoon ¼ of the veggie mixture into a cake pan. Add a layer of lasagna noodles on top, breaking apart noodles first to fit pan. Then, top with 1/3 of ricotta mixture and ¼ of mozzarella cheese. Repeat the layer 2 more times, finishing with mozzarella cheese on top. Cover cake pan with aluminum foil.
3. Place cake pan in the frying basket and Bake for 12 minutes. Remove the foil and cook for 3 more minutes. Let rest for 10 minutes before slicing. Serve immediately sprinkled with the remaining fresh basil.

Sushi-style Deviled Eggs

Servings:4

Cooking Time: 20 Minutes

Ingredients:

- ¼ cup crabmeat, shells discarded
- 4 eggs
- 2 tbsp mayonnaise
- ½ tsp soy sauce
- ¼ avocado, diced
- ¼ tsp wasabi powder
- 2 tbsp diced cucumber
- 1 sheet nori, sliced
- 8 jarred pickled ginger slices
- 1 tsp toasted sesame seeds
- 2 spring onions, sliced

Directions:

1. Preheat air fryer to 260ºF. Place the eggs in muffin cups to avoid bumping around and cracking during the cooking process. Add silicone cups to the frying basket and Air Fry for 15 minutes. Remove and plunge the eggs immediately into an ice bath to cool, about 5 minutes. Carefully peel and slice them in half lengthwise. Spoon yolks into a separate medium bowl and arrange white halves on a large plate. Mash the yolks with a fork. Stir in mayonnaise, soy sauce, avocado, and wasabi powder until smooth. Mix in cucumber and spoon into white halves. Scatter eggs with crabmeat, nori, pickled ginger, spring onions and sesame seeds to serve.

Lentil Fritters

Servings: 9

Cooking Time: 12 Minutes

Ingredients:

- 1 cup cooked red lentils
- 1 cup riced cauliflower
- ½ medium zucchini, shredded (about 1 cup)
- ¼ cup finely chopped onion
- ¼ teaspoon salt
- ¼ teaspoon black pepper

- ½ teaspoon garlic powder
- ¼ teaspoon paprika
- 1 large egg
- ⅓ cup quinoa flour

Directions:

1. Preheat the air fryer to 370°F.
2. In a large bowl, mix the lentils, cauliflower, zucchini, onion, salt, pepper, garlic powder, and paprika. Mix in the egg and flour until a thick dough forms.
3. Using a large spoon, form the dough into 9 large fritters.
4. Liberally spray the air fryer basket with olive oil. Place the fritters into the basket, leaving space around each fritter so you can flip them.
5. Cook for 6 minutes, flip, and cook another 6 minutes.
6. Remove from the air fryer and repeat with the remaining fritters. Serve warm with desired sauce and sides.

Cheddar Stuffed Portobellos With Salsa

Servings: 4
Cooking Time: 20 Minutes
Ingredients:

- 8 portobello mushrooms
- 1/3 cup salsa
- ½ cup shredded cheddar
- 2 tbsp cilantro, chopped

Directions:

1. Preheat air fryer to 370°F. Remove the mushroom stems. Divide the salsa between the caps. Top with cheese and sprinkle with cilantro. Place the mushrooms in the greased frying basket and Bake for 8-10 minutes. Let cool slightly, then serve.

Smoky Sweet Potato Fries

Servings: 4
Cooking Time: 25 Minutes
Ingredients:

- 2 large sweet potatoes, peeled and sliced
- 1 tbsp olive oil
- Salt and pepper to taste
- ¼ tsp garlic powder
- ¼ tsp smoked paprika
- 1 tbsp pumpkin pie spice
- 1 tbsp chopped parsley

Directions:

1. Preheat air fryer to 375°F. Toss sweet potato slices, olive oil, salt, pepper, garlic powder, pumpkin pie spice and paprika in a large bowl. Arrange the potatoes in a single layer in the frying basket. Air Fry for 5 minutes, then shake the basket. Air Fry for another 5 minutes and shake the basket again. Air Fry for 2-5 minutes until crispy. Serve sprinkled with parsley and enjoy.

Falafel

Servings: 4
Cooking Time: 10 Minutes
Ingredients:

- 1 cup dried chickpeas
- ½ onion, chopped
- 1 clove garlic
- ¼ cup fresh parsley leaves
- 1 teaspoon salt
- ¼ teaspoon crushed red pepper flakes
- 1 teaspoon ground cumin
- ½ teaspoon ground coriander
- 1 to 2 tablespoons flour
- olive oil
- Tomato Salad
- 2 tomatoes, seeds removed and diced
- ½ cucumber, finely diced
- ¼ red onion, finely diced and rinsed with water
- 1 teaspoon red wine vinegar
- 1 tablespoon olive oil
- salt and freshly ground black pepper
- 2 tablespoons chopped fresh parsley

Directions:

1. Cover the chickpeas with water and let them soak overnight on the counter. Then drain the chickpeas and put

them in a food processor, along with the onion, garlic, parsley, spices and 1 tablespoon of flour. Pulse in the food processor until the mixture has broken down into a coarse paste consistency. The mixture should hold together when you pinch it. Add more flour as needed, until you get this consistency.

2. Scoop portions of the mixture (about 2 tablespoons in size) and shape into balls. Place the balls on a plate and refrigerate for at least 30 minutes. You should have between 12 and 14 balls.
3. Preheat the air fryer to 380°F.
4. Spray the falafel balls with oil and place them in the air fryer. Air-fry for 10 minutes, rolling them over and spraying them with oil again halfway through the cooking time so that they cook and brown evenly.
5. Serve with pita bread, hummus, cucumbers, hot peppers, tomatoes or any other fillings you might like.

Balsamic Caprese Hasselback

Servings:4

Cooking Time: 15 Minutes

Ingredients:

- 4 tomatoes
- 12 fresh basil leaves
- 1 ball fresh mozzarella
- Salt and pepper to taste
- 1 tbsp olivc oil
- 2 tsp balsamic vinegar
- 1 tbsp basil, torn

Directions:

1. Preheat air fryer to 325ºF. Remove the bottoms from the tomatoes to create a flat surface. Make 4 even slices on each tomato, 3/4 of the way down. Slice the mozzarella and the cut into 12 pieces. Stuff 1 basil leaf and a piece of mozzarella into each slice. Sprinkle with salt and pepper. Place the stuffed tomatoes in the frying basket and Air Fry for 3 minutes. Transfer to a large serving plate. Drizzle with olive oil and balsamic vinegar and scatter the basil over. Serve and enjoy!

Veggie Burgers

Servings: 4

Cooking Time: 15 Minutes

Ingredients:

- 2 cans black beans, rinsed and drained
- ½ cup cooked quinoa
- ½ cup shredded raw sweet potato
- ¼ cup diced red onion
- 2 teaspoons ground cumin
- 1 teaspoon coriander powder
- ½ teaspoon salt
- oil for misting or cooking spray
- 8 slices bread
- suggested toppings: lettuce, tomato, red onion, Pepper Jack cheese, guacamole

Directions:

1. In a medium bowl, mash the beans with a fork.
2. Add the quinoa, sweet potato, onion, cumin, coriander, and salt and mix well with the fork.
3. Shape into 4 patties, each ¾-inch thick.
4. Mist both sides with oil or cooking spray and also mist the basket.
5. Cook at 390°F for 15minutes.
6. Follow the recipe for Toast, Plain & Simple.
7. Pop the veggie burgers back in the air fryer for a minute or two to reheat if necessary.
8. Serve on the toast with your favorite burger toppings.

Zucchini Tamale Pie

Servings: 4

Cooking Time: 45 Minutes

Ingredients:

- 1 cup canned diced tomatoes with juice
- 1 zucchini, diced
- 3 tbsp safflower oil
- 1 cup cooked pinto beans
- 3 garlic cloves, minced
- 1 tbsp corn masa flour
- 1 tsp dried oregano
- ½ tsp ground cumin
- 1 tsp onion powder
- Salt to taste
- ½ tsp red chili flakes
- ½ cup ground cornmeal
- 1 tsp nutritional yeast

- 2 tbsp chopped cilantro
- ½ tsp lime zest

Directions:

1. Warm 2 tbsp of the oil in a skillet over medium heat and sauté the zucchini for 3 minutes or until they begin to brown. Add the beans, tomatoes, garlic, flour, oregano, cumin, onion powder, salt, and chili flakes. Cook over medium heat, stirring often, about 5 minutes until the mix is thick and no liquid remains. Remove from heat. Spray a baking pan with oil and pour the mix inside. Smooth out the top and set aside.
2. In a pot over high heat, add the cornmeal, 1 ½ cups of water, and salt. Whisk constantly as the mix begins to boil. Once it boils, reduce the heat to low. Add the yeast and oil and continue to cook, stirring often, for 10 minutes or until the mix is thick and hard to stir. Remove. Preheat air fryer to 325°F. Add the cilantro and lime zest into the cornmeal mix and thoroughly combine. Using a rubber spatula, spread it evenly over the filling in the baking pan to form a crust topping. Put in the frying basket and Bake for 20 minutes or until the top is golden. Let it cool for 5 to 10 minutes, then cut and serve.

Authentic Mexican Esquites

Servings: 4

Cooking Time: 25 Minutes

Ingredients:

- 4 ears of corn, husk and silk removed
- 1 tbsp ground coriander
- 1 tbsp smoked paprika
- 1 tsp sea salt
- 1 tsp garlic powder
- 1 tsp onion powder
- 1 tsp dried lime peel
- 1 tsp cayenne pepper
- 3 tbsp mayonnaise
- 3 tbsp grated Cotija cheese
- 1 tbsp butter, melted
- 1 tsp epazote seasoning

Directions:

1. Preheat the air fryer to 400°F. Combine the coriander, paprika, salt, garlic powder, onion powder, lime peel, epazote and cayenne pepper in a small bowl and mix well. Pour into a small glass jar. Put the corn in the greased frying basket and Bake for 6-8 minutes or until the corn is crispy but tender. Make sure to rearrange the ears halfway through cooking.
2. While the corn is frying, combine the mayonnaise, cheese, and melted butter in a small bowl. Spread the mixture over the cooked corn, return to the fryer, and Bake for 3-5 minutes more or until the corn has brown spots. Remove from the fryer and sprinkle each cob with about ½ tsp of the spice mix.

Roasted Vegetable Pita Pizza

Servings: 4

Cooking Time: 20 Minutes

Ingredients:

- 1 medium red bell pepper, seeded and cut into quarters
- 1 teaspoon extra-virgin olive oil
- ⅛ teaspoon black pepper
- ⅛ teaspoon salt
- Two 6-inch whole-grain pita breads
- 6 tablespoons pesto sauce
- ¼ small red onion, thinly sliced
- ½ cup shredded part-skim mozzarella cheese

Directions:

1. Preheat the air fryer to 400°F.
2. In a small bowl, toss the bell peppers with the olive oil, pepper, and salt.
3. Place the bell peppers in the air fryer and cook for 15 minutes, shaking every 5 minutes to prevent burning.
4. Remove the peppers and set aside. Turn the air fryer temperature down to 350°F.
5. Lay the pita bread on a flat surface. Cover each with half the pesto sauce; then top with even portions of the red bell peppers and onions. Sprinkle cheese over the top. Spray the air fryer basket with olive oil mist.
6. Carefully lift the pita bread into the air fryer basket with a spatula.
7. Cook for 5 to 8 minutes, or until the outer edges begin to brown and the cheese is melted.
8. Serve warm with desired sides.

Green Bean & Baby Potato Mix

Servings: 4
Cooking Time: 25 Minutes
Ingredients:

- 1 lb baby potatoes, halved
- 4 garlic cloves, minced
- 2 tbsp olive oil
- Salt and pepper to taste
- ½ tsp hot paprika
- ½ tbsp taco seasoning
- 1 tbsp chopped parsley
- ½ lb green beans, trimmed

Directions:

1. Preheat air fryer to 375°F. Toss potatoes, garlic, olive oil, salt, pepper, hot paprika, and taco seasoning in a large bowl. Arrange the potatoes in a single layer in the air fryer basket. Air Fry for 10 minutes, then stir in green beans. Air Fry for another 10 minutes. Serve hot sprinkled with parsley.

Vegetable Hand Pies

Servings: 8
Cooking Time: 10 Minutes Per Batch
Ingredients:

- ¾ cup vegetable broth
- 8 ounces potatoes
- ¾ cup frozen chopped broccoli, thawed
- ¼ cup chopped mushrooms
- 1 tablespoon cornstarch
- 1 tablespoon milk
- 1 can organic flaky biscuits (8 large biscuits)
- oil for misting or cooking spray

Directions:

1. Place broth in medium saucepan over low heat.
2. While broth is heating, grate raw potato into a bowl of water to prevent browning. You will need ¾ cup grated potato.
3. Roughly chop the broccoli.
4. Drain potatoes and put them in the broth along with the broccoli and mushrooms. Cook on low for 5 minutes.
5. Dissolve cornstarch in milk, then stir the mixture into the broth. Cook about a minute, until mixture thickens a little. Remove from heat and cool slightly.
6. Separate each biscuit into 2 rounds. Divide vegetable mixture evenly over half the biscuit rounds, mounding filling in the center of each.
7. Top the four rounds with filling, then the other four rounds and crimp the edges together with a fork.
8. Spray both sides with oil or cooking spray and place 4 pies in a single layer in the air fryer basket.
9. Cook at 330°F for approximately 10 minutes.
10. Repeat with the remaining biscuits. The second batch may cook more quickly because the fryer will be hot.

Vegetarian Stuffed Bell Peppers

Servings: 3
Cooking Time: 40 Minutes
Ingredients:

- 1 cup mushrooms, chopped
- 1 tbsp allspice
- ¾ cup Alfredo sauce
- ½ cup canned diced tomatoes
- 1 cup cooked rice
- 2 tbsp dried parsley
- 2 tbsp hot sauce
- Salt and pepper to taste
- 3 large bell peppers

Directions:

1. Preheat air fryer to 375°F. Whisk mushrooms, allspice and 1 cup of boiling water until smooth. Stir in Alfredo sauce, tomatoes and juices, rice, parsley, hot sauce, salt, and black pepper. Set aside. Cut the top of each bell pepper, take out the core and seeds without breaking the pepper. Fill each pepper with the rice mixture and cover them with a 6-inch square of aluminum foil, folding the edges. Roast for 30 minutes until tender. Let cool completely before unwrapping. Serve immediately.

Zucchini & Bell Pepper Stir-fry

Servings: 4
Cooking Time: 25 Minutes
Ingredients:

- 1 zucchini, cut into rounds
- 1 red bell pepper, sliced
- 3 garlic cloves, sliced
- 2 tbsp olive oil
- 1/3 cup vegetable broth
- 1 tbsp lemon juice
- 2 tsp cornstarch
- 1 tsp dried basil
- Salt and pepper to taste

Directions:

1. Preheat the air fryer to 400°F. Combine the veggies, garlic, and olive oil in a bowl. Put the bowl in the frying basket and Air Fry the zucchini mixture for 5 minutes, stirring once; drain. While the veggies are cooking, whisk the broth, lemon juice, cornstarch, basil, salt, and pepper in a bowl. Pour the broth into the bowl along with the veggies and stir. Air Fry for 5-9 more minutes until the veggies are tender and the sauce is thick. Serve and enjoy!

Corn And Pepper Jack Chile Rellenos With Roasted Tomato Sauce

Servings: 3
Cooking Time: 30 Minutes
Ingredients:

- 3 Poblano peppers
- 1 cup all-purpose flour*
- salt and freshly ground black pepper
- 2 eggs, lightly beaten
- 1 cup plain breadcrumbs*
- olive oil, in a spray bottle
- Sauce
- 2 cups cherry tomatoes
- 1 Jalapeño pepper, halved and seeded
- 1 clove garlic
- ¼ red onion, broken into large pieces
- 1 tablespoon olive oil
- salt, to taste
- 2 tablespoons chopped fresh cilantro
- Filling
- olive oil
- ¼ red onion, finely chopped
- 1 teaspoon minced garlic
- 1 cup corn kernels, fresh or frozen
- 2 cups grated pepper jack cheese

Directions:

1. Start by roasting the peppers. Preheat the air fryer to 400°F. Place the peppers into the air fryer basket and air-fry at 400°F for 10 minutes, turning them over halfway through the cooking time. Remove the peppers from the basket and cover loosely with foil.
2. While the peppers are cooling, make the roasted tomato sauce. Place all sauce Ingredients except for the cilantro into the air fryer basket and air-fry at 400°F for 10 minutes, shaking the basket once or twice. When the sauce Ingredients have finished air-frying, transfer everything to a blender or food processor and blend or process to a smooth sauce, adding a little warm water to get the desired consistency. Season to taste with salt, add the cilantro and set aside.
3. While the sauce Ingredients are cooking in the air fryer, make the filling. Heat a skillet on the stovetop over medium heat. Add the olive oil and sauté the red onion and garlic for 4 to 5 minutes. Transfer the onion and garlic to a bowl, stir in the corn and cheese, and set aside.
4. Set up a dredging station with three shallow dishes. Place the flour, seasoned with salt and pepper, in the first shallow dish. Place the eggs in the second dish, and fill the third shallow dish with the breadcrumbs. When the peppers have cooled, carefully slice into one side of the pepper to create an opening. Pull the seeds out of the peppers and peel away the skins, trying not to tear the pepper. Fill each pepper with some of the corn and cheese filling and close the pepper up again by folding one side of the opening over the other. Carefully roll each pepper in the seasoned flour, then into the egg and finally into the breadcrumbs to coat on all sides, trying not to let the pepper fall open. Spray the peppers on all sides with a little olive oil.
5. Air-fry two peppers at a time at 350°F for 6 minutes. Turn the peppers over and air-fry for another 4 minutes. Serve the peppers warm on a bed of the roasted tomato sauce.

Pizza Eggplant Rounds

Servings: 4

Cooking Time: 25 Minutes

Ingredients:

- 3 tsp olive oil
- ¼ cup diced onion
- ½ tsp garlic powder
- ½ tsp dried oregano
- ½ cup diced mushrooms
- ½ cup marinara sauce
- 1 eggplant, sliced
- 1 tsp salt
- 1 cup shredded mozzarella
- 2 tbsp Parmesan cheese
- ¼ cup chopped basil

Directions:

1. Warm 2 tsp of olive oil in a skillet over medium heat. Add in onion and mushrooms and cook for 5 minutes until the onions are translucent. Stir in marinara sauce, then add oregano and garlic powder. Turn the heat off.
2. Preheat air fryer at 375ºF. Rub the remaining olive oil over both sides of the eggplant circles. Lay circles on a large plate and sprinkle with salt and black pepper. Top each circle with the marinara sauce mixture and shredded mozzarella and Parmesan cheese. Place eggplant circles in the frying basket and Bake for 5 minutes. Scatter with the basil and serve.

Fried Potatoes With Bell Peppers

Servings: 4

Cooking Time: 30 Minutes

Ingredients:

- 3 russet potatoes, cubed
- 1 tbsp canola oil
- 1 tbsp olive oil
- 1 tsp paprika
- Salt and pepper to taste
- 1 chopped shallot
- ½ chopped red bell peppers
- ½ diced yellow bell peppers

Directions:

1. Preheat air fryer to 370°F. Whisk the canola oil, olive oil, paprika, salt, and pepper in a bowl. Toss in the potatoes to coat. Place the potatoes in the air fryer and Bake for 20 minutes, shaking the basket periodically. Top the potatoes with shallot and bell peppers and cook for an additional 3-4 minutes or until the potatoes are cooked through and the peppers are soft. Serve warm.

Vegetable Side Dishes Recipes

Almond Green Beans

Servings: 4
Cooking Time: 20 Minutes

Ingredients:

- 2 cups green beans, trimmed
- ¼ cup slivered almonds
- 2 tbsp butter, melted
- Salt and pepper to taste
- 2 tsp lemon juice
- Lemon zest and slices

Directions:

1. Preheat air fryer at 375ºF. Add almonds to the frying basket and Air Fry for 2 minutes, tossing once. Set aside in a small bowl. Combine the remaining ingredients, except 1 tbsp of butter, in a bowl.
2. Place green beans in the frying basket and Air Fry for 10 minutes, tossing once. Then, transfer them to a large serving dish. Scatter with the melted butter, lemon juice and roasted almonds and toss. Serve immediately garnished with lemon zest and lemon slices.

Southern Okra Chips

Servings: 2
Cooking Time: 20 Minutes

Ingredients:

- 2 eggs
- ¼ cup whole milk
- ¼ cup bread crumbs
- ¼ cup cornmeal
- 1 tbsp Cajun seasoning
- Salt and pepper to taste
- ⅛ tsp chili pepper
- ½ lb okra, sliced
- 1 tbsp butter, melted

Directions:

1. Preheat air fryer at 400ºF. Beat the eggs and milk in a bowl. In another bowl, combine the remaining ingredients, except okra and butter. Dip okra chips in the egg mixture, then dredge them in the breadcrumbs mixture. Place okra chips in the greased frying basket and Roast for 7 minutes, shake once and brush with melted butter. Serve right away.

Honey-mustard Asparagus Puffs

Servings: 4
Cooking Time: 35 Minutes

Ingredients:

- 8 asparagus spears
- ½ sheet puff pastry
- 2 tbsp honey mustard
- 1 egg, lightly beaten

Directions:

1. Preheat the air fryer to 375°F. Spread the pastry with honey mustard and cut it into 8 strips. Wrap the pastry, honey mustard–side in, around the asparagus. Put a rack in the frying basket and lay the asparagus spears on the rack. Brush all over pastries with beaten egg and Air Fry for 12-17 minutes or until the pastry is golden. Serve.

Smashed Fried Baby Potatoes

Servings: 3
Cooking Time: 18 Minutes

Ingredients:

- 1½ pounds baby red or baby Yukon gold potatoes
- ¼ cup butter, melted
- 1 teaspoon olive oil
- ½ teaspoon paprika
- 1 teaspoon dried parsley
- salt and freshly ground black pepper
- 2 scallions, finely chopped

Directions:

1. Bring a large pot of salted water to a boil. Add the potatoes and boil for 18 minutes or until the potatoes are fork-tender.
2. Drain the potatoes and transfer them to a cutting board to cool slightly. Spray or brush the bottom of a drinking glass with a little oil. Smash or flatten the potatoes by pressing the glass down on each potato slowly. Try not to completely flatten the potato or smash it so hard that it breaks apart.
3. Combine the melted butter, olive oil, paprika, and parsley together.
4. Preheat the air fryer to 400°F.

5. Spray the bottom of the air fryer basket with oil and transfer one layer of the smashed potatoes into the basket. Brush with some of the butter mixture and season generously with salt and freshly ground black pepper.

6. Air-fry at 400°F for 10 minutes. Carefully flip the potatoes over and air-fry for an additional 8 minutes until crispy and lightly browned.

7. Keep the potatoes warm in a 170°F oven or tent with aluminum foil while you cook the second batch. Sprinkle minced scallions over the potatoes and serve warm.

Roasted Cauliflower With Garlic And Capers

Servings: 3

Cooking Time: 10 Minutes

Ingredients:

- 3 cups (about 15 ounces) 1-inch cauliflower florets
- 2 tablespoons Olive oil
- 1½ tablespoons Drained and rinsed capers, chopped
- 2 teaspoons Minced garlic
- ¼ teaspoon Table salt
- Up to ¼ teaspoon Red pepper flakes

Directions:

1. Preheat the air fryer to 375°F .

2. Stir the cauliflower florets, olive oil, capers, garlic, salt, and red pepper flakes in a large bowl until the florets are evenly coated.

3. When the machine is at temperature, put the florets in the basket, spreading them out to as close to one layer as you can. Air-fry for 10 minutes, tossing once to get any covered pieces exposed to the air currents, until tender and lightly browned.

4. Dump the contents of the basket into a serving bowl or onto a serving platter. Cool for a minute or two before serving.

Cauliflower

Servings: 4

Cooking Time: 6 Minutes

Ingredients:

- ½ cup water
- 1 10-ounce package frozen cauliflower (florets)
- 1 teaspoon lemon pepper seasoning

Directions:

1. Pour the water into air fryer drawer.
2. Pour the frozen cauliflower into the air fryer basket and sprinkle with lemon pepper seasoning.
3. Cook at 390°F for approximately 6 minutes.

Roasted Bell Peppers With Garlic & Dill

Servings: 4

Cooking Time: 30 Minutes

Ingredients:

- 4 bell peppers, seeded and cut into fourths
- 1 tsp olive oil
- 4 garlic cloves, minced
- ½ tsp dried dill

Directions:

1. Preheat air fryer to 350°F. Add the peppers to the frying basket, spritz with olive oil, shake, and Roast for 15 minutes. Season with garlic and dill, then cook for an additional 3-5 minutes. The veggies should be soft. Serve.

Roasted Fennel Salad

Servings: 3

Cooking Time: 20 Minutes

Ingredients:

- 3 cups (about ¾ pound) Trimmed fennel (see the headnote), roughly chopped
- 1½ tablespoons Olive oil
- ¼ teaspoon Table salt
- ¼ teaspoon Ground black pepper
- 1½ tablespoons White balsamic vinegar (see here)

Directions:

1. Preheat the air fryer to 400°F.

2. Toss the fennel, olive oil, salt, and pepper in a large bowl until the fennel is well coated in the oil.

3. When the machine is at temperature, pour the fennel into the basket, spreading it out into as close to one layer as possible. Air-fry for 20 minutes, tossing and rearranging the fennel pieces twice so that any covered or touching parts get exposed to the air currents, until golden at the edges and softened.

4. Pour the fennel into a serving bowl. Add the vinegar while hot. Toss well, then cool a couple of minutes before serving. Or serve at room temperature.

Rosemary Roasted Potatoes With Lemon

Cooking Time: 12 Minutes

Servings: 4

Ingredients:

- 1 pound small red-skinned potatoes, halved or cut into bite-sized chunks
- 1 tablespoon olive oil
- 1 teaspoon finely chopped fresh rosemary
- ¼ teaspoon salt
- freshly ground black pepper
- 1 tablespoon lemon zest

Directions:

1. Preheat the air fryer to 400°F.
2. Toss the potatoes with the olive oil, rosemary, salt and freshly ground black pepper.
3. Air-fry for 12 minutes (depending on the size of the chunks), tossing the potatoes a few times throughout the cooking process.
4. As soon as the potatoes are tender to a knifepoint, toss them with the lemon zest and more salt if desired.

Brussels Sprouts

Serving: 3

Cooking Time: 5 Minutes

Ingredients:

- 1 10-ounce package frozen brussels sprouts, thawed and halved
- 2 teaspoons olive oil
- salt and pepper

Directions:

1. Toss the brussels sprouts and olive oil together.
2. Place them in the air fryer basket and season to taste with salt and pepper.
3. Cook at 360°F for approximately 5minutes, until the edges begin to brown.

Herby Roasted Cherry Tomatoes

Servings: 4

Cooking Time: 20 Minutes

Ingredients:

- 1 tbsp dried oregano
- 1 tbsp dried basil
- 2 tsp dried marjoram
- 1 tsp dried thyme
- 1 tsp salt
- 2 tbsp balsamic vinegar
- 20 cherry tomatoes
- 1 tbsp olive oil

Directions:

1. Preheat the air fryer to 400°F. Combine the oregano, basil, marjoram, thyme, and salt in a small bowl and mix well. Pout into a small glass jar. Poke each cherry tomato with a toothpick to prevent bursting. Put the tomatoes, balsamic vinegar and olive oil on a piece of aluminum foil and sprinkle with 1½ tsp of the herb mix; toss. Wrap the foil around the tomatoes, leaving air space in the packet, and seal loosely. Put the packet in the air fryer and Bake for 8-10 minutes or until the tomatoes are tender.

Mashed Potato Pancakes

Servings: 6

Cooking Time: 10 Minutes

Ingredients:

- 2 cups leftover mashed potatoes
- ½ cup grated cheddar cheese
- ¼ cup thinly sliced green onions
- ½ teaspoon salt
- ¼ teaspoon black pepper
- 1 cup breadcrumbs

Directions:

1. Preheat the air fryer to 380°F.
2. In a large bowl, mix together the potatoes, cheese, and onions. Using a ¼ cup measuring cup, measure out 6 patties.

Form the potatoes into ½-inch thick patties. Season the patties with salt and pepper on both sides.

3. In a small bowl, place the breadcrumbs. Gently press the potato pancakes into the breadcrumbs.

4. Place the potato pancakes into the air fryer basket and spray with cooking spray. Cook for 5 minutes, turn the pancakes over, and cook another 3 to 5 minutes or until golden brown on the outside and cooked through on the inside.

Garlicky Bell Pepper Mix

Servings: 4

Cooking Time: 30 Minutes

Ingredients:

- 2 tbsp vegetable oil
- ½ tsp dried cilantro
- 1 red bell pepper
- 1 yellow bell pepper
- 1 orange bell pepper
- 1 green bell pepper
- Salt and pepper to taste
- 1 head garlic

Directions:

1. Preheat air fryer to 330°F. Slice the peppers into 1-inch strips. Transfer them to a large bowl along with 1 tbsp of vegetable oil. Toss to coat. Season with cilantro, salt, and pepper. Cut the top of a garlic head and place it cut-side up on an oiled square of aluminium foil. Drizzle with vegetable oil and wrap completely in the foil.

2. Roast the wrapped garlic in the air fryer for 15 minutes. Next, add the pepper strips and roast until the peppers are tender and the garlic is soft, 6-8 minutes. Transfer the peppers to a serving dish. Remove the garlic and unwrap the foil carefully. Once cooled, squeeze the cloves out of the garlic head and mix into the peppers' dish. Serve.

Layered Mixed Vegetables

Servings: 4

Cooking Time: 30 Minutes

Ingredients:

- 1 Yukon Gold potato, sliced
- 1 eggplant, sliced
- 1 carrot, thinly sliced
- ¼ cup minced onions
- 3 garlic cloves, minced
- ¾ cup milk
- 2 tbsp cornstarch
- ½ tsp dried thyme

Directions:

1. Preheat air fryer to 380°F. In layers, add the potato, eggplant, carrot, onion, and garlic to a baking pan. Combine the milk, cornstarch, and thyme in a bowl, then pour this mix over the veggies. Put the pan in the air fryer and Bake for 15 minutes. The casserole should be golden on top with softened veggies. Serve immediately.

Basic Corn On The Cob

Servings: 4

Cooking Time: 15 Minutes

Ingredients:

- 3 ears of corn, shucked and halved
- 2 tbsp butter, melted
- Salt and pepper to taste
- 1 tsp minced garlic
- 1 tsp paprika

Directions:

1. Preheat air fryer at 400ºF. Toss all ingredients in a bowl. Place corn in the frying basket and Bake for 7 minutes, turning once. Serve immediately.

Smoked Avocado Wedges

Servings:4

Cooking Time: 15 Minutes

Ingredients:

- ½ tsp smoked paprika
- 2 tsp olive oil
- ½ lime, juiced
- 8 peeled avocado wedges
- 1 tsp chipotle powder
- ¼ tsp salt

Directions:

1. Preheat air fryer to 400ºF. Drizzle the avocado wedges with olive oil and lime juice. In a bowl, combine chipotle powder, smoked paprika, and salt. Sprinkle over the avocado wedges. Place them in the frying basket and Air Fry for 7 minutes. Serve immediately.

Steak Fries

Cooking Time: 20 Minutes
Servings: 4

Ingredients:

- 2 russet potatoes, scrubbed and cut into wedges lengthwise
- 1 tablespoon olive oil
- 2 teaspoons seasoning salt (recipe below)

Directions:

1. Preheat the air fryer to 400°F.
2. Toss the potatoes with the olive oil and the seasoning salt.
3. Air-fry for 20 minutes (depending on the size of the wedges), turning the potatoes over gently a few times throughout the cooking process to brown and cook them evenly.

Summer Watermelon And Cucumber Salad

Servings: 4
Cooking Time: 15 Minutes

Ingredients:

- ½ red onion, sliced into half-moons
- 2 tbsp crumbled goat cheese
- 10 chopped basil leaves
- 4 cups watermelon cubes
- ½ cucumber, sliced
- 4 tsp olive oil
- Salt and pepper to taste
- 3 cups arugula
- 1 tsp balsamic vinegar
- 1 tsp honey
- 1 tbsp chopped mint

Directions:

1. Preheat air fryer at 375ºF. Toss watermelon, cucumber, onion, 2 tsp of olive oil, salt, and pepper in a bowl. Place it in the frying basket and Air Fry for 4 minutes, tossing once. In a salad bowl, whisk the arugula, balsamic vinegar, honey, and the remaining olive oil until the arugula is coated. Add in watermelon mixture. Scatter with goat cheese, basil leaves and mint to serve.

Cheesy Potato Pot

Servings: 4
Cooking Time: 13 Minutes

Ingredients:

- 3 cups cubed red potatoes (unpeeled, cut into ½-inch cubes)
- ½ teaspoon garlic powder
- salt and pepper
- 1 tablespoon oil
- chopped chives for garnish (optional)
- Sauce
- 2 tablespoons milk
- 1 tablespoon butter
- 2 ounces sharp Cheddar cheese, grated
- 1 tablespoon sour cream

Directions:

1. Place potato cubes in large bowl and sprinkle with garlic, salt, and pepper. Add oil and stir to coat well.
2. Cook at 390°F for 13 minutes or until potatoes are tender. Stir every 4 or 5minutes during cooking time.
3. While potatoes are cooking, combine milk and butter in a small saucepan. Warm over medium-low heat to melt butter. Add cheese and stir until it melts. The melted cheese will remain separated from the milk mixture. Remove from heat until potatoes are done.
4. When ready to serve, add sour cream to cheese mixture and stir over medium-low heat just until warmed. Place cooked potatoes in serving bowl. Pour sauce over potatoes and stir to combine.
5. Garnish with chives if desired.

Dauphinoise (potatoes Au Gratin)

Servings: 4

Cooking Time: 30 Minutes

Ingredients:

- ½ cup grated cheddar cheese
- 3 peeled potatoes, sliced
- ½ cup milk
- ½ cup heavy cream
- Salt and pepper to taste
- 1 tsp ground nutmeg

Directions:

1. Preheat air fryer to 350°F. Place the milk, heavy cream, salt, pepper, and nutmeg in a bowl and mix well. Dip in the potato slices and arrange on a baking dish. Spoon the remaining mixture over the potatoes. Scatter the grated cheddar cheese on top. Place the baking dish in the air fryer and Bake for 20 minutes. Serve warm and enjoy!

Cheesy Potato Skins

Servings: 6

Cooking Time: 54 Minutes

Ingredients:

- 3 6- to 8-ounce small russet potatoes
- 3 Thick-cut bacon strips, halved widthwise (gluten-free, if a concern)
- ¾ teaspoon Mild paprika
- ¼ teaspoon Garlic powder
- ¼ teaspoon Table salt
- ¼ teaspoon Ground black pepper
- ½ cup plus 1 tablespoon (a little over 2 ounces) Shredded Cheddar cheese
- 3 tablespoons Thinly sliced trimmed chives
- 6 tablespoons (a little over 1 ounce) Finely grated Parmesan cheese

Directions:

1. Preheat the air fryer to 375°F .
2. Prick each potato in four places with a fork (not four places in a line but four places all around the potato). Set the potatoes in the basket with as much air space between them as possible. Air-fry undisturbed for 45 minutes, or until the potatoes are tender when pricked with a fork.
3. Use kitchen tongs to gently transfer the potatoes to a wire rack. Cool for 15 minutes. Maintain the machine's temperature.
4. Lay the bacon strip halves in the basket in one layer. They may touch but should not overlap. Air-fry undisturbed for 5 minutes, until crisp. Use those same tongs to transfer the bacon pieces to the wire rack. If there's a great deal of rendered bacon fat in the basket's bottom or on a tray under the basket attachment, pour this into a bowl, cool, and discard. Don't throw it down the drain!
5. Cut the potatoes in half lengthwise (not just slit them open but actually cut in half). Use a flatware spoon to scoop the hot, soft middles into a bowl, leaving ½ inch of potato all around the inside of the spud next to the skin. Sprinkle the inside of the potato "shells" evenly with paprika, garlic powder, salt, and pepper.
6. Chop the bacon pieces into small bits. Sprinkle these along with the Cheddar and chives evenly inside the potato shells. Crumble 2 to 3 tablespoons of the soft potato insides over the filling mixture. Divide the grated Parmesan evenly over the tops of the potatoes.
7. Set the stuffed potatoes in the basket with as much air space between them as possible. Air-fry undisturbed for 4 minutes, until the cheese melts and lightly browns.
8. Use kitchen tongs to gently transfer the stuffed potato halves to a wire rack. Cool for 5 minutes before serving.

Spiced Roasted Acorn Squash

Servings: 2

Cooking Time: 45 Minutes

Ingredients:

- ½ acorn squash half
- 1 tsp butter, melted
- 2 tsp light brown sugar
- 1/8 tsp ground cinnamon
- 2 tbsp hot sauce
- ¼ cup maple syrup

Directions:

1. Preheat air fryer at 400ºF. Slice off about ¼-inch from the side of the squash half to sit flat like a bowl. In a bowl, combine all ingredients. Brush over the top of the squash and pour any remaining mixture in the middle of the squash. Place squash in the frying basket and Roast for 35 minutes. Cut it in half and divide between 2 serving plates. Serve.

Onion Rings

Servings: 4
Cooking Time: 12 Minutes

Ingredients:

- 1 large onion (preferably Vidalia or 1015)
- ½ cup flour, plus 2 tablespoons
- ½ teaspoon salt
- ½ cup beer, plus 2 tablespoons
- 1 cup crushed panko breadcrumbs
- oil for misting or cooking spray

Directions:

1. Peel onion, slice, and separate into rings.
2. In a large bowl, mix together the flour and salt. Add beer and stir until it stops foaming and makes a thick batter.
3. Place onion rings in batter and stir to coat.
4. Place breadcrumbs in a sealable plastic bag or container with lid.
5. Working with a few at a time, remove onion rings from batter, shaking off excess, and drop into breadcrumbs. Shake to coat, then lay out onion rings on cookie sheet or wax paper.
6. When finished, spray onion rings with oil or cooking spray and pile into air fryer basket.
7. Cook at 390°F for 5minutes. Shake basket and mist with oil. Cook 5minutes and mist again. Cook an additional 2 minutes, until golden brown and crispy.

Creole Potato Wedges

Servings: 4
Cooking Time: 10 Minutes

Ingredients:

- 1 pound medium Yukon gold potatoes
- ½ teaspoon cayenne pepper
- ½ teaspoon thyme
- ½ teaspoon garlic powder
- ½ teaspoon salt
- ½ teaspoon smoked paprika
- 1 cup dry breadcrumbs
- oil for misting or cooking spray

Directions:

1. Wash potatoes, cut into thick wedges, and drop wedges into a bowl of water to prevent browning.
2. Mix together the cayenne pepper, thyme, garlic powder, salt, paprika, and breadcrumbs and spread on a sheet of wax paper.
3. Remove potatoes from water and, without drying them, roll in the breadcrumb mixture.
4. Spray air fryer basket with oil or cooking spray and pile potato wedges into basket. It's okay if they form more than a single layer.
5. Cook at 390°F for 8minutes. Shake basket, then continue cooking for 2 minutes longer, until coating is crisp and potato centers are soft. Total cooking time will vary, depending on thickness of potato wedges.

Famous Potato Au Gratin

Servings: 4
Cooking Time: 35 Minutes

Ingredients:

- 2 russet potatoes, sliced
- ½ cup grated Gruyère cheese
- 2 tbsp Parmesan cheese
- ½ cup half-and-half
- 2 eggs
- 1 tbsp flour
- 1 garlic clove minced
- Salt and pepper to taste
- 1 tsp smoked paprika
- 1 cup diced cooked ham
- 1 tbsp butter, melted
- 1 tbsp bread crumbs
- 1 tbsp cilantro, chopped

Directions:

1. Combine the half-and-half, eggs, flour, salt, garlic, pepper, and paprika in a bowl Toss in potatoes until all sides of potato slices are coated. Preheat air fryer at 375ºF. Add half of the potato slices to a greased baking pan and pour half of the egg mixture. Top with ham and Gruyère cheese; then repeat the process with the remaining ingredients. Whisk the butter, Parmesan cheese, breadcrumbs, and cilantro in a bowl. Pour over casserole and cover with aluminum foil. Place baking pan in the fryer. Bake for 15 minutes. Uncover and cook for 5 more minutes. Let rest for 10 minutes before serving.

Blistered Tomatoes

Servings: 20
Cooking Time: 15 Minutes
Ingredients:

- 1½ pounds Cherry or grape tomatoes
- Olive oil spray
- 1½ teaspoons Balsamic vinegar
- ¼ teaspoon Table salt
- ¼ teaspoon Ground black pepper

Directions:

1. Put the basket in a drawer-style air fryer, or a baking tray in the lower third of a toaster oven–style air fryer. Place a 6-inch round cake pan in the basket or on the tray for a small batch, a 7-inch round cake pan for a medium batch, or an 8-inch round cake pan for a large one. Heat the air fryer to 400°F with the pan in the basket. When the machine is at temperature, keep heating the pan for 5 minutes more.
2. Place the tomatoes in a large bowl, coat them with the olive oil spray, toss gently, then spritz a couple of times more, tossing after each spritz, until the tomatoes are glistening.
3. Pour the tomatoes into the cake pan and air-fry undisturbed for 10 minutes, or until they split and begin to brown.
4. Use kitchen tongs and a nonstick-safe spatula, or silicone baking mitts, to remove the cake pan from the basket. Toss the hot tomatoes with the vinegar, salt, and pepper. Cool in the pan for a few minutes before serving.

Street Corn

Servings: 4
Cooking Time: 10 Minutes
Ingredients:

- 1 tablespoon butter
- 4 ears corn
- ⅓ cup plain Greek yogurt
- 2 tablespoons Parmesan cheese
- ½ teaspoon paprika
- ½ teaspoon garlic powder
- ¼ teaspoon salt
- ¼ teaspoon black pepper
- ¼ cup finely chopped cilantro

Directions:

1. Preheat the air fryer to 400°F.
2. In a medium microwave-safe bowl, melt the butter in the microwave. Lightly brush the outside of the ears of corn with the melted butter.
3. Place the corn into the air fryer basket and cook for 5 minutes, flip the corn, and cook another 5 minutes.
4. Meanwhile, in a medium bowl, mix the yogurt, cheese, paprika, garlic powder, salt, and pepper. Set aside.
5. Carefully remove the corn from the air fryer and let cool 3 minutes. Brush the outside edges with the yogurt mixture and top with fresh chopped cilantro. Serve immediately.

Simple Baked Potatoes With Dill Yogurt

Servings: 4
Cooking Time: 45 Minutes
Ingredients:

- 4 Yukon gold potatoes
- Salt and black pepper
- ½ cup Greek yogurt
- ¼ cup minced dill

Directions:

1. Pierce the potatoes with a fork. Lightly coat them with sprays of cooking oil, then season with salt. Preheat air fryer to 400°F. Air Fry the potatoes in the greased frying basket for 30-35 minutes, flipping once halfway through cooking until completely cooked and slightly crispy. A knife will cut into the center of the potato with ease. Remove them to a serving dish. Add toppings of yogurt, dill, salt, and pepper to taste.

Sweet Potato Curly Fries

Servings: 4

Cooking Time: 10 Minutes

Ingredients:

- 2 medium sweet potatoes, washed
- 2 tablespoons avocado oil
- ¾ teaspoon salt, divided
- 1 medium avocado
- ½ teaspoon garlic powder
- ½ teaspoon paprika
- ¼ teaspoon black pepper
- ½ juice lime
- 3 tablespoons fresh cilantro

Directions:

1. Preheat the air fryer to 400°F.
2. Using a spiralizer, create curly spirals with the sweet potatoes. Keep the pieces about 1½ inches long. Continue until all the potatoes are used.
3. In a large bowl, toss the curly sweet potatoes with the avocado oil and ½ teaspoon of the salt.
4. Place the potatoes in the air fryer basket and cook for 5 minutes; shake and cook another 5 minutes.
5. While cooking, add the avocado, garlic, paprika, pepper, the remaining ¼ teaspoon of salt, lime juice, and cilantro to a blender and process until smooth. Set aside.
6. When cooking completes, remove the fries and serve warm with the lime avocado sauce.

Desserts And Sweets

Honey Apple-pear Crisp

Servings: 4

Cooking Time: 25 Minutes

Ingredients:

- 1 peeled apple, chopped
- 2 peeled pears, chopped
- 2 tbsp honey
- ½ cup oatmeal
- 1/3 cup flour
- 3 tbsp sugar
- 2 tbsp butter, softened
- ½ tsp ground cinnamon

Directions:

1. Preheat air fryer to 380°F. Combine the apple, pears, and honey in a baking pan. Mix the oatmeal, flour, sugar, butter, and cinnamon in a bowl. Note that this mix won't be smooth. Dust the mix over the fruit, then Bake for 10-12 minutes. Serve hot.

Strawberry Donuts

Servings: 4

Cooking Time: 55 Minutes

Ingredients:

- ¾ cup Greek yogurt
- 2 tbsp maple syrup
- 1 tbsp vanilla extract
- 2 tsp active dry yeast
- 1 ½ cups all-purpose flour
- 3 tbsp milk
- ½ cup strawberry jam

Directions:

1. Preheat air fryer to 350°F. Whisk the Greek yogurt, maple syrup, vanilla extract, and yeast until well combined. Then toss in flour until you get a sticky dough. Let rest covered for 10 minutes. Flour a parchment paper on a flat surface, lay the dough, sprinkle with some flour, and flatten to ½-inch thick with a rolling pin.
2. Using a 3-inch cookie cutter, cut the donuts. Repeat the process until no dough is left. Place the donuts in the basket and let rise for 15-20 minutes. Spread some milk on top of each donut and Air Fry for 4 minutes. Turn the donuts,

spread more milk, and Air Fry for 4 more minutes until golden brown. Let cool for 15 minutes. Using a knife, cut the donuts 3/4 lengthwise, brush 1 tbsp of strawberry jam on each and close them. Serve.

Banana-almond Delights

Servings: 4
Cooking Time: 30 Minutes
Ingredients:

- 1 ripe banana, mashed
- 1 tbsp almond liqueur
- ½ tsp ground cinnamon
- 2 tbsp coconut sugar
- 1 cup almond flour
- ¼ tsp baking soda
- 8 raw almonds

Directions:

1. Preheat air fryer to 300°F. Add the banana to a bowl and stir in almond liqueur, cinnamon, and coconut sugar until well combined. Toss in almond flour and baking soda until smooth. Make 8 balls out of the mixture. Place the balls onto the parchment-lined frying basket, flatten each into ½-inch thick, and press 1 almond into the center. Bake for 12 minutes, turn and Bake for 6 more minutes. Let cool slightly before serving.

Dark Chocolate Peanut Butter S'mores

Servings: 4
Cooking Time: 6 Minutes
Ingredients:

- 4 graham cracker sheets
- 4 marshmallows
- 4 teaspoons chunky peanut butter
- 4 ounces dark chocolate
- ½ teaspoon ground cinnamon

Directions:

1. Preheat the air fryer to 390°F. Break the graham crackers in half so you have 8 pieces.
2. Place 4 pieces of graham cracker on the bottom of the air fryer. Top each with one of the marshmallows and bake for 6 or 7 minutes, or until the marshmallows have a golden brown center.
3. While cooking, slather each of the remaining graham crackers with 1 teaspoon peanut butter.
4. When baking completes, carefully remove each of the graham crackers, add 1 ounce of dark chocolate on top of the marshmallow, and lightly sprinkle with cinnamon. Top with the remaining peanut butter graham cracker to make the sandwich. Serve immediately.

Carrot-oat Cake Muffins

Servings: 4
Cooking Time: 20 Minutes
Ingredients:

- 3 tbsp butter, softened
- ¼ cup brown sugar
- 1 tbsp maple syrup
- 1 egg white
- ½ tsp vanilla extract
- 1/3 cup finely grated carrots
- ½ cup oatmeal
- 1/3 cup flour
- ½ tsp baking soda
- ¼ cup raisins

Directions:

1. Preheat air fryer to 350°F. Mix the butter, brown sugar, and maple syrup until smooth, then toss in the egg white, vanilla, and carrots. Whisk well and add the oatmeal, flour, baking soda, and raisins. Divide the mixture between muffin cups. Bake in the fryer for 8-10 minutes.

Holiday Peppermint Cake

Servings: 4

Cooking Time: 20 Minutes

Ingredients:

- 1 ½ cups flour
- 3 eggs
- 1/3 cup molasses
- ½ cup olive oil
- ½ cup almond milk
- ½ tsp vanilla extract
- ½ tsp peppermint extract
- 1 tsp baking powder
- ½ tsp salt

Directions:

1. Preheat air fryer to 380°F. Whisk the eggs and molasses in a bowl until smooth. Slowly mix in the olive oil, almond milk, and vanilla and peppermint extracts until combined. Sift the flour, baking powder, and salt in another bowl. Gradually incorporate the dry ingredients into the wet ingredients until combined. Pour the batter into a greased baking pan and place in the fryer. Bake for 12-15 minutes until a toothpick inserted in the center comes out clean. Serve and enjoy!

Baked Stuffed Pears

Servings: 4

Cooking Time: 15 Minutes + Cooling Time

Ingredients:

- 4 cored pears, halved
- ½ cup chopped cashews
- ½ cup dried cranberries
- ¼ cup agave nectar
- ½ stick butter, softened
- ½ tsp ground cinnamon
- ½ cup apple juice

Directions:

1. Preheat the air fryer to 350°F. Combine the cashews, cranberries, agave nectar, butter, and cinnamon and mix well. Stuff this mixture into the pears, heaping it up on top. Set the pears in a baking pan and pour the apple juice into the bottom of the pan. Put the pan in the fryer and Bake for 10-12 minutes or until the pears are tender. Let cool before serving.

Thumbprint Sugar Cookies

Servings: 10

Cooking Time: 8 Minutes

Ingredients:

- 2½ tablespoons butter
- ⅓ cup cane sugar
- 1 teaspoon pure vanilla extract
- 1 large egg
- 1 cup all-purpose flour
- ½ teaspoon baking soda
- ¼ teaspoon salt
- 10 chocolate kisses

Directions:

1. Preheat the air fryer to 350°F.
2. In a large bowl, cream the butter with the sugar and vanilla. Whisk in the egg and set aside.
3. In a separate bowl, mix the flour, baking soda, and salt. Then gently mix the dry ingredients into the wet. Portion the dough into 10 balls; then press down on each with the bottom of a cup to create a flat cookie.
4. Liberally spray the metal trivet of an air fryer basket with olive oil mist.
5. Place the cookies in the air fryer basket on the trivet and cook for 8 minutes or until the tops begin to lightly brown.
6. Remove and immediately press the chocolate kisses into the tops of the cookies while still warm.
7. Let cool 5 minutes and then enjoy.

Honey-pecan Yogurt Cake

Servings: 6

Cooking Time: 18-24 Minutes

Ingredients:

- 1 cup plus 3½ tablespoons All-purpose flour
- ¼ teaspoon Baking powder
- ¼ teaspoon Baking soda
- ¼ teaspoon Table salt
- 5 tablespoons Plain full-fat, low-fat, or fat-free Greek yogurt

- 5 tablespoons Honey
- 5 tablespoons Pasteurized egg substitute, such as Egg Beaters
- 2 teaspoons Vanilla extract
- ⅔ cup Chopped pecans
- Baking spray (see here)

Directions:

1. Preheat the air fryer to 325°F (or 330°F, if the closest setting).
2. Mix the flour, baking powder, baking soda, and salt in a small bowl until well combined.
3. Using an electric hand mixer at medium speed , beat the yogurt, honey, egg substitute or egg, and vanilla in a medium bowl until smooth, about 2 minutes, scraping down the inside of the bowl once or twice.
4. Turn off the mixer; scrape down and remove the beaters. Fold in the flour mixture with a rubber spatula, just until all of the flour has been moistened. Fold in the pecans until they are evenly distributed in the mixture.
5. Use the baking spray to generously coat the inside of a 6-inch round cake pan for a small batch, a 7-inch round cake pan for a medium batch, or an 8-inch round cake pan for a large batch. Scrape and spread the batter into the pan, smoothing the batter out to an even layer.
6. Set the pan in the basket and air-fry for 18 minutes for a 6-inch layer, 22 minutes for a 7-inch layer, or 24 minutes for an 8-inch layer, or until a toothpick or cake tester inserted into the center of the cake comes out clean. Start checking it at the 15-minute mark to know where you are.
7. Use hot pads or silicone baking mitts to transfer the cake pan to a wire rack. Cool for 5 minutes. To unmold, set a cutting board over the baking pan and invert both the board and the pan. Lift the still-warm pan off the cake layer. Set the wire rack on top of that layer and invert all of it with the cutting board so that the cake layer is now right side up on the wire rack. Remove the cutting board and continue cooling the cake for at least 10 minutes or to room temperature, about 30 minutes, before slicing into wedges.

Peanut Butter-banana Roll-ups

Servings: 4

Cooking Time: 20 Minutes

Ingredients:

- 2 ripe bananas, halved crosswise
- 4 spring roll wrappers
- ¼ cup molasses
- ¼ cup peanut butter
- 1 tsp ground cinnamon
- 1 tsp lemon zest

Directions:

1. Preheat air fryer to 375°F. Place the roll wrappers on a flat surface with one corner facing up. Spread 1 tbsp of molasses on each, then 1 tbsp of peanut butter, and finally top with lemon zest and 1 banana half. Sprinkle with cinnamon all over. For the wontons, fold the bottom over the banana, then fold the sides, and roll-up. Place them seam-side down and Roast for 10 minutes until golden brown and crispy. Serve warm.

Pumpkin Brownies

Servings: 4

Cooking Time: 30 Minutes

Ingredients:

- ¼ cup canned pumpkin
- ½ cup maple syrup
- 2 eggs, beaten
- 1 tbsp vanilla extract
- ¼ cup tapioca flour
- ¼ cup flour
- ½ tsp baking powder

Directions:

1. Preheat air fryer to 320°F. Mix the pumpkin, maple syrup, eggs, and vanilla extract in a bowl. Toss in tapioca flour, flour, and baking powder until smooth. Pour the batter into a small round cake pan and Bake for 20 minutes until a toothpick comes out clean. Let cool completely before slicing into 4 brownies. Serve and enjoy!

Brown Sugar Baked Apples

Servings: 4

Cooking Time: 15 Minutes

Ingredients:

- 3 Small tart apples, preferably McIntosh
- 4 tablespoons (¼ cup/½ stick) Butter
- 6 tablespoons Light brown sugar
- Ground cinnamon
- Table salt

Directions:

1. Preheat the air fryer to 400°F.
2. Stem the apples, then cut them in half through their "equators" (that is, not the stem ends). Use a melon baller to core the apples, taking care not to break through the flesh and skin at any point but creating a little well in the center of each half.
3. When the machine is at temperature, remove the basket and set it on a heat-safe work surface. Set the apple halves cut side up in the basket with as much air space between them as possible. Even a fraction of an inch will work. Drop 2 teaspoons of butter into the well in the center of each apple half. Sprinkle each half with 1 tablespoon brown sugar and a pinch each ground cinnamon and table salt.
4. Return the basket to the machine. Air-fry undisturbed for 15 minutes, or until the apple halves have softened and the brown sugar has caramelized.
5. Use a nonstick-safe spatula to transfer the apple halves cut side up to a wire rack. Cool for at least 10 minutes before serving, or serve at room temperature.

Cinnamon Pear Cheesecake

Servings: 6

Cooking Time: 60 Minutes + Cooling Time

Ingredients:

- 16 oz cream cheese, softened
- 1 cup crumbled graham crackers
- 4 peeled pears, sliced
- 1 tsp vanilla extract
- 1 tbsp brown sugar
- 1 tsp ground cinnamon
- 1 egg
- 1 cup condensed milk
- 2 tbsp white sugar
- 1 ½ tsp butter, melted

Directions:

1. Preheat air fryer to 350°F. Place the crumbled graham cracker, white sugar, and butter in a large bowl and stir to combine. Spoon the mixture into a greased pan and press around the edges to flatten it against the dish. Place the pan into the frying basket and Bake for 5 minutes. Remove and let it cool for 30 minutes to harden.
2. Place the cream cheese, vanilla extract, brown sugar, cinnamon, condensed milk and egg in a large bowl and whip until the ingredients are thoroughly mixed. Arrange the pear slices on the cooled crust and spoon the wet mixture over. Level the top with a spatula. Place the pan in the frying basket. Bake for 40 minutes. Allow to cool completely. Serve and enjoy!

Home-style Pumpkin Pie Pudding

Servings: 4

Cooking Time: 30 Minutes

Ingredients:

- 1 cup canned pumpkin purée
- ¼ cup sugar
- 3 tbsp all-purpose flour
- 1 tbsp butter, melted
- 1 egg
- 1 orange, zested
- 2 tbsp milk
- 1 tsp vanilla extract
- 4 vanilla wafers, crumbled

Directions:

1. Preheat air fryer to 350°F. Beat the pumpkin puree, sugar, flour, butter, egg, orange zest, milk, and vanilla until well-mixed. Spritz a baking pan with the cooking spray, then pour the pumpkin mix in. Place it in the air fryer and Bake for 11-17 minutes or until golden brown. Take the pudding out of the fryer and let it chill. Serve with vanilla wager crumbs.

Orange-chocolate Cake

Servings: 6

Cooking Time: 35 Minutes

Ingredients:

- ¾ cup flour
- ½ cup sugar
- 7 tbsp cocoa powder
- ½ tsp baking soda
- ½ cup milk
- 2 ½ tbsp sunflower oil
- ½ tbsp orange juice
- 2 tsp vanilla
- 2 tsp orange zest
- 3 tbsp butter, softened
- 1 ¼ cups powdered sugar

Directions:

1. Use a whisk to combine the flour, sugar, 2 tbsp of cocoa powder, baking soda, and a pinch of salt in a bowl. Once combined, add milk, sunflower oil, orange juice, and orange zest. Stir until combined. Preheat the air fryer to 350°F. Pour the batter into a greased cake pan and Bake for 25 minutes or until a knife inserted in the center comes out clean.
2. Use an electric beater to beat the butter and powdered sugar together in a bowl. Add the remaining cocoa powder and vanilla and whip until fluffy. Scrape the sides occasionally. Refrigerate until ready to use. Allow the cake to cool completely, then run a knife around the edges of the baking pan. Turn it upside-down on a plate so it can be frosted on the sides and top. When the frosting is no longer cold, use a butter knife or small spatula to frost the sides and top. Cut into slices and enjoy!

Raspberry Empanada

Servings: 6

Cooking Time: 35 Minutes

Ingredients:

- 1 can raspberry pie filling
- 1 puff pastry dough
- 1 egg white, beaten

Directions:

1. Preheat air fryer to 370°F. Unroll the two sheets of dough and cut into 4 squares each, or 8 squares total. Scoop ½ to 1 tbsp of the raspberry pie filling in the center of each square. Brush the edges with egg white. Fold diagonally to form a triangle and close the turnover. Press the edges with the back of a fork to seal. Arrange the turnovers in a single layer in the greased basket. Spray the empanadas with cooking oil and Bake for 8 minutes. Let them sit in the air fryer for 3-4 minutes to cool before removing. Repeat for the other batch. Serve and enjoy!

Boston Cream Donut Holes

Servings: 24

Cooking Time: 12 Minutes

Ingredients:

- 1½ cups bread flour
- 1 teaspoon active dry yeast
- 1 tablespoon sugar
- ¼ teaspoon salt
- ½ cup warm milk
- ½ teaspoon pure vanilla extract
- 2 egg yolks
- 2 tablespoons butter, melted
- vegetable oil
- Custard Filling:
- 1 (3.4-ounce) box French vanilla instant pudding mix
- ¾ cup whole milk
- ¼ cup heavy cream
- Chocolate Glaze:
- 1 cup chocolate chips
- ⅓ cup heavy cream

Directions:

1. Combine the flour, yeast, sugar and salt in the bowl of a stand mixer. Add the milk, vanilla, egg yolks and butter. Mix until the dough starts to come together in a ball. Transfer the dough to a floured surface and knead the dough by hand for 2 minutes. Shape the dough into a ball, place it in a large oiled bowl, cover the bowl with a clean kitchen towel and let the dough rise for 1 to 1½ hours or until the dough has doubled in size.
2. When the dough has risen, punch it down and roll it into a 24-inch log. Cut the dough into 24 pieces and roll each piece into a ball. Place the dough balls on a baking sheet and let them rise for another 30 minutes.
3. Preheat the air fryer to 400°F.

4. Spray or brush the dough balls lightly with vegetable oil and air-fry eight at a time for 4 minutes, turning them over halfway through the cooking time.
5. While donut holes are cooking, make the filling and chocolate glaze. To make the filling, use an electric hand mixer to beat the French vanilla pudding, milk and ¼ cup of heavy cream together for 2 minutes.
6. To make the chocolate glaze, place the chocolate chips in a medium-sized bowl. Bring the heavy cream to a boil on the stovetop and pour it over the chocolate chips. Stir until the chips are melted and the glaze is smooth.
7. To fill the donut holes, place the custard filling in a pastry bag with a long tip. Poke a hole into the side of the donut hole with a small knife. Wiggle the knife around to make room for the filling. Place the pastry bag tip into the hole and slowly squeeze the custard into the center of the donut. Dip the top half of the donut into the chocolate glaze, letting any excess glaze drip back into the bowl. Let the glazed donut holes sit for a few minutes before serving.

Cinnamon Tortilla Crisps

Servings: 4
Cooking Time: 8 Minutes
Ingredients:

- 1 tortilla
- 2 tsp muscovado sugar
- ½ tsp cinnamon

Directions:

1. Preheat air fryer to 350°F. Slice the tortilla into 8 triangles like a pizza. Put the slices on a plate and spray both sides with oil. Sprinkle muscovado sugar and cinnamon on top, then lightly spray the tops with oil. Place in the frying basket in a single layer. Air Fry for 5-6 minutes or until they are light brown. Enjoy warm.

Molten Chocolate Almond Cakes

Servings: 3
Cooking Time: 13 Minutes
Ingredients:

- butter and flour for the ramekins
- 4 ounces bittersweet chocolate, chopped
- ½ cup (1 stick) unsalted butter
- 2 eggs
- 2 egg yolks
- ¼ cup sugar
- ½ teaspoon pure vanilla extract, or almond extract
- 1 tablespoon all-purpose flour
- 3 tablespoons ground almonds
- 8 to 12 semisweet chocolate discs (or 4 chunks of chocolate)
- cocoa powder or powdered sugar, for dusting
- toasted almonds, coarsely chopped

Directions:

1. Butter and flour three (6-ounce) ramekins. (Butter the ramekins and then coat the butter with flour by shaking it around in the ramekin and dumping out any excess.)
2. Melt the chocolate and butter together, either in the microwave or in a double boiler. In a separate bowl, beat the eggs, egg yolks and sugar together until light and smooth. Add the vanilla extract. Whisk the chocolate mixture into the egg mixture. Stir in the flour and ground almonds.
3. Preheat the air fryer to 330°F.
4. Transfer the batter carefully to the buttered ramekins, filling halfway. Place two or three chocolate discs in the center of the batter and then fill the ramekins to ½-inch below the top with the remaining batter. Place the ramekins into the air fryer basket and air-fry at 330°F for 13 minutes. The sides of the cake should be set, but the centers should be slightly soft. Remove the ramekins from the air fryer and let the cakes sit for 5 minutes. (If you'd like the cake a little less molten, air-fry for 14 minutes and let the cakes sit for 4 minutes.)
5. Run a butter knife around the edge of the ramekins and invert the cakes onto a plate. Lift the ramekin off the plate slowly and carefully so that the cake doesn't break. Dust with cocoa powder or powdered sugar and serve with a scoop of ice cream and some coarsely chopped toasted almonds.

Coconut-custard Pie

Servings: 4

Cooking Time: 20 Minutes

Ingredients:

- 1 cup milk
- ¼ cup plus 2 tablespoons sugar
- ¼ cup biscuit baking mix
- 1 teaspoon vanilla
- 2 eggs
- 2 tablespoons melted butter
- cooking spray
- ½ cup shredded, sweetened coconut

Directions:

1. Place all ingredients except coconut in a medium bowl.
2. Using a hand mixer, beat on high speed for 3minutes.
3. Let sit for 5minutes.
4. Preheat air fryer to 330°F.
5. Spray a 6-inch round or 6 x 6-inch square baking pan with cooking spray and place pan in air fryer basket.
6. Pour filling into pan and sprinkle coconut over top.
7. Cook pie at 330°F for 20 minutes or until center sets.

Orange Gooey Butter Cake

Servings: 6

Cooking Time: 85 Minutes

Ingredients:

- Crust Layer:
- ½ cup flour
- ¼ cup sugar
- ½ teaspoon baking powder
- ⅛ teaspoon salt
- 2 ounces (½ stick) unsalted European style butter, melted
- 1 egg
- 1 teaspoon orange extract
- 2 tablespoons orange zest
- Gooey Butter Layer:
- 8 ounces cream cheese, softened
- 4 ounces (1 stick) unsalted European style butter, melted
- 2 eggs
- 2 teaspoons orange extract
- 2 tablespoons orange zest
- 4 cups powdered sugar
- Garnish:
- powdered sugar
- orange slices

Directions:

1. Preheat the air fryer to 350°F.
2. Grease a 7-inch cake pan and line the bottom with parchment paper. Combine the flour, sugar, baking powder and salt in a bowl. Add the melted butter, egg, orange extract and orange zest. Mix well and press this mixture into the bottom of the greased cake pan. Lower the pan into the basket using an aluminum foil sling (fold a piece of aluminum foil into a strip about 2-inches wide by 24-inches long). Fold the ends of the aluminum foil over the top of the dish before returning the basket to the air fryer. Air-fry uncovered for 8 minutes.
3. To make the gooey butter layer, beat the cream cheese, melted butter, eggs, orange extract and orange zest in a large bowl using an electric hand mixer. Add the powdered sugar in stages, beat until smooth with each addition. Pour this mixture on top of the baked crust in the cake pan. Wrap the pan with a piece of greased aluminum foil, tenting the top of the foil to leave a little room for the cake to rise.
4. Air-fry for 60 minutes at 350°F. Remove the aluminum foil and air-fry for an additional 17 minutes.
5. Let the cake cool inside the pan for at least 10 minutes. Then, run a butter knife around the cake and let the cake cool completely in the pan. When cooled, run the butter knife around the edges of the cake again and invert it onto a plate and then back onto a serving platter. Sprinkle the powdered sugar over the top of the cake and garnish with orange slices.

Cherry Cheesecake Rolls

Servings: 6

Cooking Time: 30 Minutes

Ingredients:

- 1 can crescent rolls
- 4 oz cream cheese
- 1 tbsp cherry preserves
- 1/3 cup sliced fresh cherries

Directions:

1. Roll out the dough into a large rectangle on a flat work surface. Cut the dough into 12 rectangles by cutting 3 cuts

across and 2 cuts down. In a microwave-safe bowl, soften cream cheese for 15 seconds. Stir together with cherry preserves. Mound 2 tsp of the cherries-cheese mix on each piece of dough. Carefully spread the mixture but not on the edges. Top with 2 tsp of cherries each. Roll each triangle to make a cylinder.

2. Preheat air fryer to 350°F. Place the first batch of the rolls in the greased air fryer. Spray the rolls with cooking oil and Bake for 8 minutes. Let cool in the air fryer for 2-3 minutes before removing. Serve.

Caramel Blondies With Macadamia Nuts

Servings: 4

Cooking Time: 35 Minutes + Cooling Time

Ingredients:

- 1/3 cup ground macadamia
- ½ cup unsalted butter
- 1 cup white sugar
- 1 tsp vanilla extract
- 2 eggs
- ½ cup all-purpose flour
- ½ cup caramel chips
- ¼ tsp baking powder
- A pinch of salt

Directions:

1. Preheat air fryer to 340°F. Whisk the eggs in a bowl. Add the melted butter and vanilla extract and whip thoroughly until slightly fluffy. Combine the flour, sugar, ground macadamia, caramel chips, salt, and baking powder in another bowl. Slowly pour the dry ingredients into the wet ingredients, stirring until thoroughly blended and until there are no lumps in the batter. Spoon the batter into a greased cake pan. Place the pan in the air fryer.Bake for 20 minutes until a knife comes out dry and clean. Let cool for a few minutes before cutting and serving.

Air-fried Beignets

Servings: 24

Cooking Time: 5 Minutes

Ingredients:

- ¾ cup lukewarm water (about 90°F)
- ¼ cup sugar
- 1 generous teaspoon active dry yeast (½ envelope)
- 3½ to 4 cups all-purpose flour
- ½ teaspoon salt
- 2 tablespoons unsalted butter, room temperature and cut into small pieces
- 1 egg, lightly beaten
- ½ cup evaporated milk
- ¼ cup melted butter
- 1 cup confectioners' sugar
- chocolate sauce or raspberry sauce, to dip

Directions:

1. Combine the lukewarm water, a pinch of the sugar and the yeast in a bowl and let it proof for 5 minutes. It should froth a little. If it doesn't froth, your yeast is not active and you should start again with new yeast.

2. Combine 3½ cups of the flour, salt, 2 tablespoons of butter and the remaining sugar in a large bowl, or in the bowl of a stand mixer. Add the egg, evaporated milk and yeast mixture to the bowl and mix with a wooden spoon (or the paddle attachment of the stand mixer) until the dough comes together in a sticky ball. Add a little more flour if necessary to get the dough to form. Transfer the dough to an oiled bowl, cover with plastic wrap or a clean kitchen towel and let it rise in a warm place for at least 2 hours or until it has doubled in size. Longer is better for flavor development and you can even let the dough rest in the refrigerator overnight (just remember to bring it to room temperature before proceeding with the recipe).

3. Roll the dough out to ½-inch thickness. Cut the dough into rectangular or diamond-shaped pieces. You can make the beignets any size you like, but this recipe will give you 24 (2-inch x 3-inch) rectangles.

4. Preheat the air fryer to 350°F.

5. Brush the beignets on both sides with some of the melted butter and air-fry in batches at 350°F for 5 minutes, turning them over halfway through if desired. (They will brown on all sides without being flipped, but flipping them will brown them more evenly.)

6. As soon as the beignets are finished, transfer them to a plate or baking sheet and dust with the confectioners' sugar. Serve warm with a chocolate or raspberry sauce.

Donut Holes

Servings: 13
Cooking Time: 12 Minutes

Ingredients:

- 6 tablespoons Granulated white sugar
- 1½ tablespoons Butter, melted and cooled
- 2 tablespoons (or 1 small egg, well beaten) Pasteurized egg substitute, such as Egg Beaters
- 6 tablespoons Regular or low-fat sour cream (not fat-free)
- ¾ teaspoon Vanilla extract
- 1⅔ cups All-purpose flour
- ¾ teaspoon Baking powder
- ¼ teaspoon Table salt
- Vegetable oil spray

Directions:

1. Preheat the air fryer to 350°F .
2. Whisk the sugar and melted butter in a medium bowl until well combined. Whisk in the egg substitute or egg , then the sour cream and vanilla until smooth. Remove the whisk and stir in the flour, baking powder, and salt with a wooden spoon just until a soft dough forms.
3. Use 2 tablespoons of this dough to create a ball between your clean palms. Set it aside and continue making balls: 8 more for the small batch, 12 more for the medium batch, or 17 more for the large one.
4. Coat the balls in the vegetable oil spray, then set them in the basket with as much air space between them as possible. Even a fraction of an inch will be enough, but they should not touch. Air-fry undisturbed for 12 minutes, or until browned and cooked through. A toothpick inserted into the center of a ball should come out clean.
5. Pour the contents of the basket onto a wire rack. Cool for at least 5 minutes before serving.

Giant Buttery Chocolate Chip Cookie

Servings: 4
Cooking Time: 16 Minutes

Ingredients:

- ⅔ cup plus 1 tablespoon All-purpose flour
- ¼ teaspoon Baking soda
- ¼ teaspoon Table salt
- Baking spray (see the headnote)
- 4 tablespoons (¼ cup/½ stick) plus 1 teaspoon Butter, at room temperature
- ¼ cup plus 1 teaspoon Packed dark brown sugar
- 3 tablespoons plus 1 teaspoon Granulated white sugar
- 2½ tablespoons Pasteurized egg substitute, such as Egg Beaters
- ½ teaspoon Vanilla extract
- ¾ cup plus 1 tablespoon Semisweet or bittersweet chocolate chips

Directions:

1. Preheat the air fryer to 350°F .
2. Whisk the flour, baking soda, and salt in a bowl until well combined.
3. For a small air fryer, coat the inside of a 6-inch round cake pan with baking spray. For a medium air fryer, coat the inside of a 7-inch round cake pan with baking spray. And for a large air fryer, coat the inside of an 8-inch round cake pan with baking spray.
4. Using a hand electric mixer at medium speed, beat the butter, brown sugar, and granulated white sugar in a bowl until smooth and thick, about 3 minutes, scraping down the inside of the bowl several times.
5. Beat in the pasteurized egg substitute or egg (as applicable) and vanilla until uniform. Scrape down and remove the beaters. Fold in the flour mixture and chocolate chips with a rubber spatula, just until combined. Scrape and gently press this dough into the prepared pan, getting it even across the pan to the perimeter.
6. Set the pan in the basket and air-fry undisturbed for 16 minutes, or until the cookie is puffed, browned, and feels set to the touch.
7. Transfer the pan to a wire rack and cool for 10 minutes. Loosen the cookie from the perimeter with a spatula, then invert the pan onto a cutting board and let the cookie come free. Remove the pan and reinvert the cookie onto the wire rack. Cool for 5 minutes more before slicing into wedges to serve.

Spanish Churro Bites

Servings: 5
Cooking Time: 35 Minutes
Ingredients:

- ¼ tsp salt
- 2 tbsp vegetable oil
- 3 tbsp white sugar
- 1 cup flour
- ½ tsp ground cinnamon
- 2 tbsp granulated sugar

Directions:

1. On the stovetop, add 1 cup of water, salt, 1 tbsp of vegetable oil and 1 tbsp sugar in a pot. Bring to a boil over high heat. Remove from the heat and add flour. Stir with a wooden spoon until the flour is combined and a ball of dough forms. Cool for 5 minutes. Put the ball of dough in a plastic pastry bag with a star tip. Squeeze the dough to the tip and twist the top of the bag. Squeeze 10 strips of dough, about 5-inches long each, onto a workspace. Spray with cooking oil.
2. Preheat air fryer to 340°F. Place the churros in the greased frying basket and Air Fry for 22-25 minutes, flipping once halfway through until golden. Meanwhile, heat the remaining vegetable oil in a small bowl. In another shallow bowl, mix the remaining 2 tbsp sugar and cinnamon. Roll the cooked churros in cinnamon sugar. Top with granulated sugar and serve immediately.

Fast Brownies

Servings: 4
Cooking Time: 25 Minutes
Ingredients:

- ½ cup flour
- 2 tbsp cocoa
- 1/3 cup granulated sugar
- ¼ tsp baking soda
- 3 tbsp butter, melted
- 1 egg
- ¼ tsp salt
- ½ cup chocolate chips
- ¼ cup chopped hazelnuts
- 1 tbsp powdered sugar
- 1 tsp vanilla extract

Directions:

1. Preheat air fryer at 350°F. Combine all ingredients, except chocolate chips, hazelnuts, and powdered sugar, in a bowl. Fold in chocolate chips and pecans. Press mixture into a greased cake pan. Place cake pan in the frying basket and Bake for 12 minutes. Let cool for 10 minutes before slicing into 9 brownies. Scatter with powdered sugar and serve.

Easy Bread Pudding

Servings: 4
Cooking Time: 25 Minutes
Ingredients:

- 2 cups sandwich bread cubes
- ½ cup pecan pieces
- ½ cup raisins
- 3 eggs
- ¼ cup half-and-half
- ¼ cup dark corn syrup
- 1 tsp vanilla extract
- 2 tbsp bourbon
- 2 tbsp dark brown sugar
- ¼ tsp ground cinnamon
- ½ tsp nutmeg
- ¼ tsp salt

Directions:

1. Preheat air fryer at 325°F. Spread the bread pieces in a cake pan and layer pecan pieces and raisins over the top. Whisk the eggs, half-and-half, corn syrup, bourbon, vanilla extract, sugar, cinnamon, nutmeg, and salt in a bowl. Pour egg mixture over pecan pieces. Let sit for 10 minutes. Place the cake pan in the frying basket and Bake for 15 minutes. Let cool onto a cooling rack for 10 minutes before slicing. Serve immediately.

RECIPES INDEX

A

B

C

D

E

F

G

H

I

K

L

M

O

P

Q

R

S

Printed in Great Britain
by Amazon